ROCK STAR

ROCK STAR

MY LIFE ON AND OFF THE ICE

JENNIFER JONES

WITH BOB WEEKS

Collins

An Imprint of HarperCollins Publishers

Rock Star
Copyright © 2025 by Jennifer Jones.
All rights reserved.

Published by Collins, an imprint of HarperCollins Publishers Ltd

FIRST EDITION

No part of this book may be used or reproduced in any manner whatsoever without written permission.

Without limiting the exclusive rights of any author, contributor or the publisher of this publication, any unauthorized use of this publication to train generative artificial intelligence (AI) technologies is expressly prohibited. HarperCollins also exercise their rights under Article 4(3) of the Digital Single Market Directive 2019/790 and expressly reserve this publication from the text and data mining exception.

HarperCollins books may be purchased for educational, business, or sales promotional use through our Special Markets Department.

HarperCollins Publishers Ltd
Bay Adelaide Centre, East Tower
22 Adelaide Street West, 41st Floor
Toronto, Ontario, Canada
M5H 4E3
www.harpercollins.ca

HarperCollins Publishers
Macken House, 39/40 Mayor Street Upper
Dublin 1, D01 C9W8, Ireland
https://www.harpercollins.com

Library and Archives Canada Cataloguing in Publication

Title: Rock star : my life on and off the ice / Jennifer Jones with Bob Weeks.
Names: Jones, Jennifer, 1974- author. | Weeks, Bob, author
Description: First edition.
Identifiers: Canadiana (print) 20250210509 | Canadiana (ebook) 2025021072X |
    ISBN 9781443474559 (hardcover) | ISBN 9781443474566 (ebook)
Subjects: LCSH: Jones, Jennifer, 1974- | LCSH: Curlers (Athletes)—Canada—
Biography. | LCSH: Women curlers—Canada—Biography. | LCSH: Curling. |
    LCGFT: Autobiographies.
Classification: LCC GV845.62.J66 A3 2025 | DDC 796.964092—dc23

Printed and bound in the United States of America

25 26 27 28 29 LBC 5 4 3 2 1

*To my beautiful daughters, Isabella and Skyla,
who completed my life and filled my heart in a way I
didn't think possible; my husband, Brent, for loving
me like no other; my stepson, Wil, for allowing me to
join his world, and my mom and dad for being the
best parents a girl could ask for. I love you more.*

CONTENTS

1.	A Farewell to Remember	1
2.	My Rocking Roots	9
3.	A Balancing Act	25
4.	A Big Part of a Small Team	35
5.	Why Not Me?	51
6.	The Shot Heard Round the World	67
7.	The World Catches Up	79
8.	Anything but Perfect	99
9.	Up Close and Too Personal	113
10.	Downhill and Uphill	123
11.	Mother and Baby	147
12.	Going for Gold	157
13.	Team Jones Way	173
14.	The Dream Team	187
15.	Skyla's Turn	207
16.	The Long and Winding Road to Beijing	225
17.	The Beijing Bubble	239
18.	Dream Big	251
19.	A Clear Mind, an Unburdened Heart	267
	Acknowledgements	273

ROCK STAR

1

A FAREWELL TO REMEMBER

I'D ALWAYS THOUGHT that when it came time to throw my last rock at the Scotties Tournament of Hearts I'd pause to savour it all and remember the moment. To smell the ice, as I always say. After all, the Canadian championship was a large part of my curling career. I played in the event 18 times, starting in 2002. Now here I was in Calgary, 22 years later, playing my final Scotties game, getting ready to throw my last stone.

People tell you to savour the moments with your children because, before you know it, they'll be grown up and you will miss those days of putting them to bed. You'll want those moments back—those stressful yet happiest times of your life. As a mom, I have always taken those words seriously and felt them deeply, which is one of the biggest reasons I decided to say goodbye to competitive curling. I wanted to spend more time with our children. However, as I approached the last few moments of my curling career, I realized those words are also true of life and its moments. Where did the time go? I often still feel

ROCK STAR

like the new kid on the block of the curling scene, but I know I'm not. I am the veteran, and it's time to pass the torch.

And yet, it feels like just yesterday that I took my first slide over the Scotties hearts emblazoned on the ice we played on. I wish someone had told me back then to savour every single second because, before you know it, you will take your last slide. My mantra has always been to enjoy the moment, and I feel I did that more than most. But I still can't believe it has been over 20 years since my first Scotties.

But the magic of the moment of my final farewell didn't unfold in the way I had always imagined. Instead of taking a meaningless shot to end a game, I found myself in one last national final, with everything on the line and only two shots left to determine the winner. I had a shot that, if we executed it perfectly, would force Team Ontario and its skip, Rachel Homan, into a very difficult draw to the four-foot to decide who would be crowned Team Canada. A shot that, if Rachel missed, would lead to a record-breaking seventh Scotties championship for me and the first Canadian championship for each of my teammates.

That's where my focus was as I slid down the ice toward the awaiting rock. There was no chance to look around or think about the end of my Scotties career. Instead, as I had done tens of thousands of times during my years on the ice, I went through my routine. I flipped the rock on its side, cleaned the bottom and returned it to the ice. I rubbed my hand on my leg and then looked down the ice at my target and focused on my throw. Time stood still, as it always does for me in those grandest of moments. I will remember that instant not for being my last shot at a Scotties but for being an important shot in an important

A FAREWELL TO REMEMBER

game. These are the moments I have always lived for. Now here I was, one last time, leaving it all on the line. Here goes nothing.

Sadly, that final shot missed by centimetres, giving the victory to the very talented Homan team. Our journey was over. Some would say the story didn't have a fairy-tale ending, but I'd say it ended the way it was meant to. And I can say, with my whole heart, that I left it all out there and I have absolutely no regrets. OK, maybe I wish the result had been different. But that's not something within my control.

Obviously, there were a few brief moments of disappointment at the outcome, but then I realized . . . it was over. As I moved down the ice to shake hands with the champions and hug my teammates, it hit me that there were no more Scotties to play in. No more clutch shots to attempt. No more team uniforms. No more opening ceremonies, or bagpipes or cheering after shots. In that moment, I wasn't sure how to handle what was happening.

Rachel and her team got a deserving wave of applause, but after a few moments I looked around and saw that everyone was standing and clapping and cheering. It was for the winners, but it became apparent that it was also for me. It didn't take long for the tears to flow in the most humbling moment I have ever experienced. My Scotties career was over, and the crowd was saying goodbye.

I was having trouble handling the emotions of the situation when my daughters, Isabella and Skyla, jumped onto the ice, ran over and hugged me. As they wrapped their arms around me, the only thing the girls said was, "Mom, please change your mind and keep curling." They just kept saying, "Please"—and looking at me with the biggest eyes. This moment marked the end of the magic not just for me but, in a lot of ways, for them too. As a mom you never want to feel like you are letting your children down, but I knew in my heart it was the right time—both for me and for my family. I held my two little angels as close and as tight as I could and soaked in that moment.

The Scotties farewell had been a whirlwind because we had focused on winning the event until the very last shot. Fortunately for me, I had the opportunity to say goodbye one more time, a few weeks later in Toronto at the Players' Championship, the final Grand Slam of Curling event of the season and, fittingly, one of my favourite events to play in. I believe that the inclusion of women in the Players' Championship was the first big step in the growth of women's curling around the world. This time, I watched the final moments, as Anna Hasselborg, the skip of the dynamic Swedish team, played a takeout on my rock to end the game—and my career in four-player curling.

Once again, the ovation erupted and I could feel the emotions welling up inside me. I remember Anna giving me a hug at the end of the game, thanking me for everything I had done for women's curling, and telling me to enjoy the moment because I deserved every single second of it. Once again, the emotion was overwhelming and tears streamed down my face, and I felt so humbled.

As I slid down the ice to grab my gripper at the other end of the sheet, the cheering grew louder. I looked around the crowd and saw lots of friends and fellow curlers, many of them teammates from over the years. Dawn McEwen, my long-time lead, had flown in to be there with me. Curlers I'd battled on the ice and been friends with off it were there as well. It was both a

A FAREWELL TO REMEMBER

humbling and an overwhelming moment that made it hard to know what to do other than acknowledge the cheers and wipe away my tears.

Both the Scotties and the Grand Slam of Curling have been integral parts of my curling career and my life. The Scotties allowed me to be a Canadian, world and Olympic champion.

The Grand Slams were the events where the women's game was really allowed to shine. They gave us a venue to be on television and fine-tune our skills so we could become champions, while showing the world what we were capable of. These two events symbolized what I was able to achieve, and going out with a chance to play both once more was wonderful and, to me, a fitting end.

The ovations I received and the messages and gratitude that overloaded my phone in the days and weeks after were somewhat surprising. I hadn't realized the impact I had had on the sport until it was over, but I've always been proud of what I've given back, whether it was how I played or how I interacted with the fans, sponsors and media.

The end of my career has given me time to reflect on the long and incredible journey that curling has taken me on. It started in Winnipeg at the St. Vital Curling Club, where my parents were members and avid curlers. The club ran a daycare in the basement of the building, where I was looked after while my parents were curling. Even back then, I was enthralled with the game, although at that point I hadn't really played. But I would sneak out of the daycare and sit up behind the glass and watch the rocks go up and down the ice. I was hooked.

A few years later, when I was 11, I played my first event, a

Christmas bonspiel at the Assiniboine Memorial Curling Club. I sported a puffy, oversized sweatshirt with a panda on the front—a far cry from the Team Canada jacket I'd wear many times in the future. I'm not sure how we did in that bonspiel, but I know I felt the rush of competition.

From those early days, curling has been a major part of my life, taking me around the world, allowing me to meet dignitaries from presidents and prime ministers to fellow athletes in different sports. I've played in championships of every level, winning some, losing others and riding the emotional wave that comes with each game and each competition.

I've been a part of exceptionally talented teams and also played on some that just didn't work, leading to the difficult task of parting ways.

I've made friendships with curlers and fans that have spanned decades, adjusted to the media spotlight (which was uncomfortable at first) and signed countless autographs and posed for thousands and thousands of photos.

I played in regional, provincial, national, global and Olympic competitions, many of them while trying to manage my job as a corporate lawyer.

Curling allowed me to grow from a shy girl who preferred to be in the back row as part of the crowd into a leader who stood at the front and made tough decisions both on and off the ice. As my profile and reputation in the sport grew, I had to learn to grow with it. I was able to help not only my team but also the sport and, specifically, the women's side of it, speaking out when things weren't fair and using my voice to advocate for changes.

A FAREWELL TO REMEMBER

Leadership was one of the biggest and hardest transformations for me, a journey that came as a result of curling and wound up having an impact on my entire life. As I leave the game on the ice, I plan to continue speaking out and helping curling—and women's sport in general—grow.

Most importantly, curling allowed me to meet my husband, Brent Laing, and his son, Wil, and to give Brent and me two wonderful daughters who are my foundation. In many ways, the commitment to my girls is the major reason I decided to stop playing four-player curling. I will still play mixed doubles with Brent, but the hectic days of training and playing with a four-player team are now behind me. My involvement in the game won't end, but it will continue in different, less demanding ways.

Looking back on my career, I now sometimes wonder, *How did I ever manage to do it all?* But as Brent always says, "There is nothing you can't do. And if it's not complicated and challenging, it's not us."

2

MY ROCKING ROOTS

WHEN I WAS growing up in Winnipeg, the centre of my family's life was the curling club. The St. Vital Curling Club, to be exact. It's a six-sheet facility where my parents, my sister, Heather, and I spent more time than we did in our own home. Or at least it seemed like that. Even to this day, walking into the St. Vital Curling Club gives me the same feeling I would get as walking into our childhood home. A sense of calm and comfort and a place that I belong.

My father, Larry, was an avid curler who started playing when he was a teenager living in Fort Frances, Ontario. His parents couldn't afford the costs associated with playing hockey, but curling, with its minimal equipment requirements and low entry fees, was fine. My dad loved the game and played a lot in his youth in Fort Frances. When his parents moved to Winnipeg, they settled in the St. Vital area and joined the curling club in that part of town.

Curling gives us friendships that last a lifetime. My dad's friends from high school were also curlers, and a group of five

ROCK STAR

of them hung out and played together on the ice for a long time. Over the years, they remained very close as they finished their schooling and went out into the working world, my dad into a career in sales. But they never left St. Vital. They all remained active in the club, and all five would go on to be presidents of the St. Vital CC, helping to guide the facility and shape its future. That's how important curling and the club were to their lives. It brought them together, and they became part of our family growing up. They were all uncles to me, and most of my childhood memories involved these incredible men. I remember as a little girl looking up at the presidents' pictures with pride as I saw my dad and my "uncles" on the wall. It was a sense of community that was beyond special to me, and something that I strive to find in my life again today.

My mother, Carol, never played the game growing up, but when she met my father, he convinced her to give it a try. Anyone who knows my mom knows she would never say no. Especially to my dad, the love of her life. I think she knew that if she was going to spend time with my dad, she'd have to start curling. So off she went with pantyhose under her polyester pants and a smile on her face. My dad bought her some learn-to-curl lessons from Ray Turnbull, who was an active teacher in the Winnipeg area and would go on to win the Brier and spend years as an analyst for TSN. Nothing but the best for my mom.

Initially, my parents played together in mixed, but after a few years, my mom joined the women's league and truly enjoyed curling and the curlers she met, who became close friends.

My mom really embraced curling, which was no surprise. She has never been afraid to try new things and always tried to live life to the fullest no matter where she was or what she was doing. Part of that, I'm sure, stems from her career as an oncology nurse and the work that involves. I've always been in awe of the strength of character she has and the outlook she carries every single day. It's been an inspiration for me. I am often asked who my role models are. That is easy. My parents. My dad for his passion, true sense of community, generosity and love of the game. My mom for her positive attitude and independence and for also enjoying every second of life.

It's also one of the reasons I gained an attitude of never being afraid to lose. Curling is important to me, but the game is about the adventure, the experience and the people, not the wins and losses. My mom made me see that in the way she lives her life.

My sister, Heather, who is a year and a half older, started curling at the same time I did. We played together in our early days as juniors and had lots of fun and some success at the club.

She was a good player and competed in a few junior provincial championships but wasn't driven to play the way I was. I have never told her this, but I think she could have won a Scotties if she'd put more time into it. But that wasn't her passion. Being my number one fan was. She has supported me without question or waver from the first moment I slid on the ice.

Before I turned 10, I spent a lot of time watching my parents curl, and from time to time, my dad would take me out on the ice, teaching me some of the fundamentals of the game. He had a very deliberate way of how he thought the curling delivery should be taught. I believe it is one of the main reasons I have experienced the success that I have. It all stems from those strong fundamentals my dad taught me from day one. However, it wasn't the conventional way 30 years ago. He certainly must have known what he was doing because the principles of what he was giving me are the same ones that David Murdoch, Canada's high-performance director, is using in his training of the country's top players today. I wish my dad were here to see it. He would be so proud.

When we weren't curling, my sister and I would sit behind the glass and watch our parents' games. Sometimes, when we got restless, we'd help the bartender wash glasses in this very cool, special-glass dishwasher. Occasionally as payment, she would give us one of those lottery tickets where you peel open tabs to see the result. On one occasion, I won $100. I remember jumping up and down knowing I could finally buy curling shoes instead of using my mom's hand-me-downs. I was 12 years old. My dad took me to Asham Curling Supplies, and I got my first new curling shoes with a red brick slider. They were perfect!

This was all well before I was allowed to be a full-fledged member. The age for a junior membership at St. Vital was 13, but because of my fervour for the game and perhaps because they had a hard time keeping me off the ice, the club allowed me to join at 11. I believe I annoyed them so much and my dad was so persistent that they finally said yes.

I just couldn't get enough of going to the club and practising or playing in a game. Because St. Vital was a busy place, the only practice time available was at 8:00 a.m. on Saturday morning. My dad would drive me there, and I was so excited to get on the ice, I'd be sitting at the door with all my gear by 7:00 a.m., waiting for him to take us. (This may be another reason why my

MY ROCKING ROOTS

sister didn't enjoy curling as much as I did—she didn't like those early wake-up calls!)

I learned so much in those early-morning sessions. My dad helped me work on my line of delivery for hours; slide after slide, over and over I'd go. Out to his broom on one side of the sheet, then the other and then down centre ice. It never felt like practice to me. I just loved being out there.

As if practising wasn't enough, I wanted to learn from watching the sport's best, and my dad and I would tape the big games on TV. We'd watch them intently, and I came to notice that many of the men's games had a lot more rocks in play than the women's. While there were certainly teams that preferred playing hits to draws, the leading men's rinks played a lot more aggressively, while many of the top women's teams were using a defensive style. Back then an open hit, which today is likely the easiest shot in the game, wasn't a guarantee, so you didn't tend to mix it up and take chances, which I found boring.

I loved watching the women's games—although there weren't many shown on television at that time—but I told my father I wanted to play like Kerry Burtnyk, Ed Werenich and Russ Howard, who were so intriguing to watch. They took risks and weren't afraid to take chances with lots of rocks in play, leading to an infinite number of strategic situations. This was also happening in the days before the free guard zone rule, which made it more impressive. For me, it seemed a lot more fun to play this way, and it was certainly a lot more fun to watch.

As I mentioned earlier, my first bonspiel was over Christmas at the Assiniboine Curling Club when I was 11. The next year I began playing in junior bonspiels around the city. In those days, the curling clubs around Winnipeg were so jammed that our events took place late at night. And by late, I mean very late. We would begin playing after the 10:00 p.m. adults' draw, which usually meant about midnight. We would go all night long, with the finals being played around dawn. Looking back, it seems crazy, but we were all young and full of energy, so it was lots of fun (although I'm not sure the parents who chaperoned us were quite as excited). Thinking back on the "all-nighters" makes me smile because we had so much fun, and only ever got into a bit of mischief, but it was always so tame and innocent. We just wanted to curl.

I got right into those bonspiels, most times playing with a team that included my sister. I loved the competition, playing key shots and analyzing the strategy. I also enjoyed playing skip and having the last rock in my hand. Some curlers may not want the pressure of having the game on the line with their final stone, but for me, there was nothing more exciting. That's something that stayed with me my entire career. I just can't imagine playing any other position.

In 1990, when I was 15, I skipped my team in the Manitoba provincial junior playdowns. The rink was made up of Tracey Lavery at third, my sister at second and Dana Malanchuk at lead. Our record wasn't great. We managed to win one game and lose two more before being eliminated. But it gave me a taste of competitive curling and I loved it. I was hooked.

At the end of that season, I got a phone call from Jill Staub (later Thurston), a top-ranked junior player who was a few years older than me. At first, I couldn't understand why she'd be calling

MY ROCKING ROOTS

me, and when she asked if I'd be interested in playing with her team the following year, my jaw just about hit the ground.

Here was one of the top players in the province, who was three years older than me, asking me to join her rink after we won just one game in provincials. She wanted me as her third, and I jumped at the offer. I told my team, who were beyond supportive. Without hesitation, my sister told me I had to get this experience. Always my number one fan.

Also on the team were Kristie Moroz, playing second, and at lead was Kelly MacKenzie. (I would play a lot against MacKenzie over the course of my career. She's better known in curling circles by her married name, Kelly Scott.)

Our team had a good season and ended up winning the Manitoba junior title. That sent us off to the Canadian championship in Leduc, Alberta. I couldn't believe it. I had earned my first "buffalo." Winning a Manitoba curling championship means you get to wear your provincial uniform at the national championship, and part of that is a big buffalo crest on the back of the jackets. For a curling kid growing up in Manitoba, it doesn't get much better than that. It was a huge step up for me but something I was so excited for. This was where I wanted to be, at the top level competing against the best not just in my city or province, but from across the country.

We played well throughout the round robin and ended up first with an impressive 10-1 record, our only loss coming to Alberta. That put us into the final against New Brunswick, which knocked off Alberta in the semifinal.

The New Brunswick rink was skipped by Heather Smith,

ROCK STAR

another player I would battle with during my years in women's curling, and she and her team gave us a real test. However, in the 10th end, we had a draw to an empty house. Hit the rings and we were Canadian champs. The shot you dream of to win a national championship. But the rock was heavy and slid through, pushing us to an extra end.

In the 11th, we had another draw, this time to the four-foot. Once again, it was just a bit heavy and slid just a few inches too deep.

I was immediately crushed and, after shaking hands with the new champions, began crying. I wasn't blaming Jill by any means; it was just the fact that we came so close and then lost. The tears wouldn't stop, and at one point, the television cameras (in those days the boys' and girls' junior championships aired live on CBC) showed me bawling as I plopped down on the carpet at the end of the sheet. Later, at the closing ceremony, I was up on the podium and still crying.

It may seem odd, but that moment is one of the most important of my career. Not the loss, but the crying and disappointment.

When I got home, every newspaper picture showed me with tears running down my cheeks, whether I was still on the ice or getting my silver medal. What it really showed me was that I was not a good teammate. I thought Jill was amazing, and she was a big part of why we were even in that final, but by being so emotional, I didn't show her support at a time she could have used it. I have never forgiven myself for that.

I was so worried about the outcome of that final and so scared to lose that game, and because of that, I didn't enjoy any of it. At that moment, I vowed to myself that I would never let

MY ROCKING ROOTS

that happen again. In any game, big or small, I would go out there and I would love it. I would soak up the atmosphere. I would certainly try my best to win, but I wouldn't be scared to lose. I would just enjoy the moment and let the result take care of itself. Most importantly, I would also never, ever cry again after losing a game, and to this day, I've never cried publicly over a loss. After all, it's just a game that we go and play and put our hearts and souls into, and if we're only playing for the wins, then we've lost the point. We've lost the love of the game. Fortunately for me, that was never a problem. I did cry after my final Scotties, but not because of the loss. Those were tears of sadness to say goodbye to a great love.

I really think that experience at my first Canadian championship all those years ago changed me as a player. It altered my perception of the teammate I wanted to be. Not being afraid to lose, in some ways, also made it easier to win. It freed me up to focus on leaving it all out on the ice and having no regrets at the end of a game. If you're scared to lose, you're getting in your own way. You're not playing the way you need to play to perform at your best. Even when we would go out and lose a game, as long as I truly left it all out there, and supported my teammates, I could leave the ice feeling OK.

The next year, Jill and Kristie became too old for junior curling, which meant putting together a new team. After getting a taste of the top levels of the game, I felt I was ready to skip, so I went about putting my own team together.

Dana had played with me the year before and was a phenomenal lead and friend. I had committed to Dana that if our team didn't win the Canadian championship, we would play together the following year. So Dana and I were looking for two other players. The first person I approached was Jill Officer. I really didn't know her that well yet, but in between games at a bonspiel at the Highlander Curling Club, I stopped her in a hallway and pulled her behind a Coke machine so no one would see us. I asked if she'd be interested in putting a team together. I was thrilled when she said yes. Neither of us knew it at that moment, but that was the start of a long and endearing friendship.

Our third was Trisha Baldwin, a very solid player I'd known for some time. Her father worked at Asham Curling Supplies and her uncle was Arnold Asham, the founder of that company. She came from a real curling family.

The four of us gelled very quickly. We all shared a drive to be great curlers and a great team.

Our first year together was a good one. We made it all the way to the final of the Manitoba juniors but lost to Tracey Lavery. Again, it was tough to lose, but we all learned a lot along the way.

In 1993, we won the Manitoba title and went off to the Canadian final in Trois-Rivières, Quebec, where we finished with an 8-4 mark and missed the playoffs.

The next season, we went full speed, knowing we were good enough to accomplish big things. We played as much as we could, not only in junior events, because there weren't too many of those, but also in women's bonspiels. The top Manitoba players of the day were always there, and it was impressive and awe-inspiring to see players such as Connie Laliberte on the next sheet.

MY ROCKING ROOTS

Stepping up to the women's level also meant a higher financial commitment in terms of entry fees and travel. We had to save money as best we could, and so we usually stayed four to a hotel room and ate cheap meals. The early days of the struggling curling-tour life.

At one bonspiel we played well enough to win $1,000, and for us, that was huge. A few events later, we won a bigger bonspiel and took home $6,000. It felt like we'd won the lottery. Most of that money went right back into paying our expenses, which also meant we could eat a little better. No more canned food on the road.

In 1994, we finally achieved what we had set out to do when we put our team together. We won the province and played the national final in Truro, Nova Scotia, getting through the round robin with a 7-4 record.

That left us in a three-way tie for third place, which meant we had to beat Northern Ontario and Ontario in tiebreakers, just to get to the semifinal, where we then got past British Columbia, putting us into the Canadian final. Another chance to become Team Canada.

In that game, we played Saskatchewan's Sherry Linton, and after a close contest for most of it, we stole single points in the ninth and 10th ends for an 8–5 win. It was even more eventful when, in the middle of the game, I slipped and hit myself in the eye with my broom on national TV. I got a black eye immediately, and I remember Trisha, fearing I was going to have to stop, saying, "You have to keep playing. I can't skip." Yes, she could, but I managed to finish the game with a black eye on top of the podium.

ROCK STAR

At long last, we were Canadian champions. We celebrated all the hard work that brought us to the top step of the podium, but the best part was winning it with my teammates, who were also great friends.

There were a few ups and downs after that win. The biggest up was that we were invited to play in the Bern Bonspiel, a major women's tournament in Switzerland that had a great international field.

For us, the biggest thrill was travelling there and hanging out with Sandra Schmirler's rink. They were the reigning Canadian and world champions and huge icons for us. They were also great in treating us as friends during the trip. In fact, it got to the point where they would play practical jokes on us, like putting plastic wrap over our toilets. You can imagine how that turned out. They also had the most beautiful charm on their necklaces, a gold curling rock. I asked them where they got it from, and the answer was Thun, Switzerland. So off I went, I had to have one. I had never been on a train before, never mind in Europe, but we made it to Thun and I purchased my most treasured gold curling rock, which was the biggest splurge of my life to that point.

For us four wide-eyed juniors, hanging with these legends was an experience we will never forget.

On the downside was a situation involving our chance to play at the world junior championship in 1995 as Team Canada, an opportunity we had earned. Up to that time, the teams winning the Canadian junior title represented Canada at the world championship the following year. But the Canadian Curling Association, now Curling Canada, decided to change plans and send the winning rink the same year.

MY ROCKING ROOTS

It meant there was going to be two champions—us from 1994 and the winner from 1995—for one spot in the 1995 world juniors. We knew the situation when we were playing the Canadian final, but at that point, no decision had been made as to how it was going to be resolved.

In a bizarre ruling, Curling Canada elected to have us go to the '95 Canadian junior championship and put us directly into the semifinal. I did appreciate that they were giving us an opportunity to win the Canadian title again so we could represent Canada at a world championship. They were in a tough spot, but I didn't agree with the approach. We arrived at the Canadian championship having played no round robin games, not having thrown a rock on the ice and not knowing anything about the conditions, going up against another team that had been competing all week. In the curling world, this was unheard of and a massive disadvantage for us.

We lobbied to try to just become another team in the round robin, playing from the start of the week. But Curling Canada turned that request down, saying it would be too complicated to organize the draw with an extra team.

We pointed out that the Scotties Tournament of Hearts had added Team Canada, the defending Canadian champions from the previous year, to the draw in 1986, so there was precedent for what we were asking. But they refused. We were more than a little frustrated and felt we'd been put at a huge disadvantage. Despite our repeated requests, we never received an explanation about how they came to their decision or how their decision could even be considered fair, other than we were getting an opportunity to play in the semifinal.

Things got even stranger when we learned we'd be playing against BC, which was skipped by Kelly MacKenzie, my former teammate, who had moved to the West Coast. Her team ended up defeating us and then going on to win both the Canadian final and, a few weeks later, the world junior championship.

We were young at the time, so it was hard not to feel we had been robbed of our chance to represent Canada. An honour that every other Canadian junior champion had been able to experience up until that year. At that point in my life, the world juniors was the big show. It was what I had dreamed of being a part of, and the whole situation didn't make any sense to me. To this day, I still can't reconcile how that decision was reached and how Curling Canada thought that was the best way to decide which team would go to the world championship. But the decision was theirs to make, and our dreams were crushed.

Still, as my junior career was coming to an end, I began to look ahead and not behind. I was moving on to women's competition. One of the most significant moments that prepared me for this transition came a couple of years earlier, in 1993, when the Scotties Tournament of Hearts was played in Brandon, Manitoba.

My coach at the time, Lyle Hudson, took some of us up to watch. I remember walking into the Keystone Centre and seeing the ice filled with some of the biggest names in the game: Colleen Jones, Connie Laliberte, Anne Merklinger and Maureen Bonar, who was representing Manitoba. The arena was packed with fans, and I looked around and thought to myself how amazing it would be to experience this just once in my life.

MY ROCKING ROOTS

The atmosphere was electric, with people cheering and players yelling sweeping orders. It was equal parts chaotic, with multiple games going on at the same time, and strangely enticing. Players sliding, others sweeping, skips yelling instructions and the big scoreboards at each end of the ice displaying the scores.

In the stands, the fans seemed to have come from every part of Canada. Many were wearing their province's colours or dressed up to signify their home province teams, so there was no doubt who they were supporting. The Nova Scotia fans put blue colouring on their noses, representing their provincial nickname of Bluenosers. Some from PEI wore hats that had red-haired pigtails flowing from them like Anne of Green Gables. Flags from every province and territory were waved back and forth. And everyone—curlers, fans and officials—seemed to be having a great time.

To me, this was nirvana. I wanted to be on the ice, throwing stones, calling shots and looking up at all these fans just having the time of their lives.

Little did I know at that point that I'd play in more than one Scotties, and that I'd compete in my first one in that same building in Brandon in just a few years.

3

A BALANCING ACT

I KNOW IT may be hard to believe, but my life at that time wasn't all about curling, even though the sport did affect some of my life choices.

Aside from my dedication to curling, I was a normal teenager, going to high school, studying hard and working at McDonald's. Yup, if you went to the Golden Arches in Windsor Park in the late 1980s, there's a good chance I gave you your Big Mac and fries. I actually worked my way up to a manager position and would work before high school started and then after school. My goals were to buy a car and to ensure I had the financial resources to chase my dreams.

I graduated in 1992, and I entered the University of Manitoba, determined to build a career. Specifically, I wanted a career that would let me curl. Initially, I thought I wanted to be a doctor, and I took sciences in my first year. I was still in junior curling at this time, and I was doing my best to balance my time between schoolwork and throwing stones.

That same year I got quite sick, and I missed a great deal

of time at school. That gave me the opportunity to think about where my life was heading and what I wanted to achieve. I was determined to keep curling at the highest levels. But I also wanted to continue my focus on trying to become a doctor. That required me to do a lot of lab work, which was time consuming, and it became more and more difficult to curl, go to school and keep working. After a lot of soul-searching, I realized there was just no way I could manage all of it.

I had to make a hard decision: Do I want to be a doctor, or do I want to curl? To some, that may seem like a strange choice, but that's how much curling meant to me. It was really the centre of my universe, and everything else revolved around that.

Not surprisingly, curling won out. But I was still intent on building a career, so I switched my focus and decided to obtain a law degree. I then began my undergraduate studies in economics and psychology. This change in academic direction gave me more freedom, and that meant more time to be on the ice and on the road to play in the big events of the day.

Over the next few years, I juggled curling and my studies and successfully obtained my undergrad degree. The next step in my plan was to take the Law School Admission Test, better known as the LSAT. I scored well and chose to attend the law school at the University of Manitoba, because it would allow me to continue to curl with my team. At that point there were no exceptions to the residency rule—even if you were going to school. Curling Canada had a rule that you must live in the same province as the rest of your team in order to compete at the Scotties. It was a rule that had been in place for many years, designed to ensure that team members were representing the province in which they were living,

A BALANCING ACT

first at the Brier and then, when the women were included, at the Scotties. However, at the time the rule was introduced, it was not common for people to move for jobs or relationships. Flying was a luxury, not something you did every week. Curling wasn't yet part of the Olympics, and the stakes were not as high. It was a different era.

Curling Canada wanted to protect the integrity and tradition of the Brier and the Scotties. As a result, the rule was not amended to keep up with the changing times. Some fans agreed because they like to cheer for their province and were resistant to change. I am not sure if they fully understood what this meant for the competitive curlers at the time and how much the rule impacted our lives. This residency rule has influenced so many decisions in my life. Curling Canada is in a tough spot, trying to balance the needs of the players while protecting the history of national championships. The association has gradually made changes to reflect the needs of players and the changing times.

Once again, there were a lot of doubters. Many of my friends just assumed I would quit curling, at least in the short term, to focus on the law degree. But I knew I was going to be able to balance both. My parents, however, were always in my corner and knew I could do it. "You've done everything you've said you were going to do your entire life," my mom said to me. "I don't know why this will be any different."

Of course, she was right. At that point in my life, even though I was still a teenager, I was driven to be independent. During the summer months, it wasn't unusual for me to have three jobs. I saved as much money as I could, and I was very frugal when I did spend any of it. By the time I turned 16, I'd made enough

ROCK STAR

money to buy my own car. It cost $4,500 at the time, and I remember how long it took me to earn it. By the time I'd reached my early 20s, I'd saved enough to make a down payment on a house. I was filled with drive and determination—that's just who I was.

A lot of my summer work also supported my curling. We needed money to enter events, travel to them and stay in hotels. I sacrificed a lot when I was in high school and university. I wanted to curl, I wanted to be successful in school and I wanted to save money. My friends and any summer adventures came fourth and fifth on that list.

That's not to say I didn't have any friends or fun at all. I've had the same best friend for my entire life. Robyn Page (later Koropatnick) lived down the street from me growing up, and we first met when we were babies. We've stayed close ever since. She has always been there no matter what. She supports my dreams, but we rarely talk about curling. We talk about everything else, which I love.

There was also a group that I started with three other friends, and it eventually expanded to 12. It became known as the $20 Club. It's not an overstatement to say it's been a key part of my life. Once a month, we'd gather at someone's house and contribute $20 each to the hostess. The next month, the person who'd been given the money would have to show us what she had purchased. There was one rule: It had to be something personal, a treat, not just paying off a bill of some sort.

When we first started, and it was my turn, I remember buying a purse and a pair of sunglasses and going for a pedicure, which was unusual and a bit difficult for me, because I didn't like to

A BALANCING ACT

spend my money on anything unnecessary. Gradually, over time, being part of this group allowed me to open up in ways I never had before.

The women in the $20 Club were great because they were always flexible with my curling schedule when they were setting dates for the next meeting. More importantly, we didn't really talk about curling. When curling season was over, I loved being with people who didn't know me as Jennifer Jones the curler and who didn't want to know why I played that certain shot in the final end of the game against Ontario in the Scotties. With these ladies, I could just be myself, and over time we all became very close. They were such a supportive group of friends, and although I didn't know it at the time, I needed those women. In my push to be independent, I had more or less isolated myself inside curling. But this group of women kept me balanced, kept me close, and I gradually opened up and began to rely on their friendships throughout the ups and downs in my life. They made me feel loved.

In many ways, the $20 Club became a big part of my curling success too. When curling fans asked, "How did you make those big shots?" I would answer that I wasn't afraid to lose. I wasn't scared of the outcome. Did I want to win? Of course. I believe I love curling more than anyone, and I love being successful at it. And I've always had teammates who knew it was OK if I missed. Now I also had a group of friends who simply didn't care if I won or lost or even curled, for that matter. They cared about me, and they let me know that life was going to be just fine no matter what the scoreboard said.

In later years, these women would come out and watch me

curl even though some of them had no idea what the rules were. It was fun to have them there, and it made me into a more welcoming person. I learned and trusted that they would be there for me whenever I needed them. That kind of unconditional friendship had been missing from my life up to that point. Over the next decade, I needed that group of women often, because they were a valuable reminder that I was more than just a curler.

Living a very one-dimensional life is not an uncommon story among top curlers and, for that matter, many elite athletes. It's easy to get wrapped up in your sport and not have an outlet beyond it. You play the sport, talk about the sport, watch the sport, have friends who play the sport, and you never get away from it. There is almost a FOMO—fear of missing out—if you don't continue to make your entire life about your sport. Eventually, if you don't have another outlet, you become smothered by it. I've seen athletes follow that singular path, and when their sports careers end, there's nothing waiting for them. It's like following a road that ends at the edge of a cliff—where do you go now?

That's almost where I was until I took a step back and learned that in some cases, less is more. To become a better player, I needed to sometimes separate myself from curling. And, more importantly, I had to become a more well-rounded person. I will always be grateful for the incredible women in the $20 Club.

WHEN LAW SCHOOL started in the fall, my narrow focus on curling and studies continued. I won't lie; it did take a lot of commitment to curl and study, especially on the road when we were all sharing a room. While my teammates would sit on the bed and watch television or listen to music, I would scoop up a couple of pillows and a blanket and stretch out in the bathtub and study. If they went out to dinner or to socialize, I always stayed back, nose in my books, trying to keep up with my work. My days had a simple order to them: curl, study, eat, sleep, repeat. It all paid off in 1999 when I graduated near the top of my class. But my double duty wasn't over. I still had my articling to do.

I was lucky enough to get matched with one of Winnipeg's top firms, Aikins, MacAulay and Thorvaldson (now MLT Aikins). I went in for an interview and met with a group that included one of the senior partners, Jim Ferguson. After I'd answered most of the standard questions, I told them I was an active curler and I'd like to be able to continue that. As anyone who has ever been an articling student can attest, the work usually doesn't allow for anything other than eating and sleeping. Aikins took me on, and somehow, I managed to do everything they asked while also keeping on top of my curling.

When the articling was over, they went a step further and asked me to stay on full time. I was told that the firm liked the way I carried myself and was impressed with my work ethic. Everyone had always told me I couldn't be a curler and a lawyer, and yet there I was, being offered a great job at the biggest law firm in Winnipeg. I would be working with Jim Ferguson, and I was thrilled.

Jim and I just hit it off. He was smart and very good at his job. It was also easy to see that his family was his top priority. I thought, here is one of the most successful lawyers in Manitoba, if not the most successful, and his family is always first. He has the best clients. He gets his work done. This is the lawyer that I want to be. This is the person I want to be. He taught me so much from a legal sense, but he also cared about me as a person. He soon became a mentor and was beyond supportive of my curling. But I also made it clear to him that my legal work would be a priority, and I would never miss a deadline.

There were times when keeping that promise was difficult. One year, I was at the world championship preparing for a semi-final game. At the same time, we were in the middle of closing a big deal back home. I spent most of the morning on a conference call, working on the deal. When the semifinal was over, I was back on the phone, continuing my day job, while also getting ready for the final.

Doing work before a world championship semifinal was a little unusual, but being on a call while I was away curling wasn't. I made a pact with Jim that no matter how much I travelled or how many games I played, I would always get my work done. We both understood there would be certain times of the day when I wouldn't be available, but I would never let him or the firm down.

Being on the road curling also meant I had a lot of catching up to do whenever I got home to Winnipeg. It wasn't unusual for me to spend 15 or 16 hours at the office when I wasn't curling. I was pretty much always the first person to arrive in the morning and the last one to leave at night. I was committed to keeping my word, and that meant ensuring I finished everything required of me in the office.

Gradually, I established myself in the Winnipeg legal community. Everyone knew I was a world-class curler, but I also

A BALANCING ACT

gained a reputation as a good lawyer. That was clear when Charlie Spiring of Wellington West approached me about coming to work for him. This time, I didn't need to disclose that I was a curler; he was well aware of my success on the ice. In fact, that was part of the attraction.

"I believe in dreamers," he said. "And I want to support your dream of being both a curler and a lawyer."

I talked with Charlie's right-hand man, Blaine Coates, and negotiated a deal. He promised me a flexible schedule that would allow me more time to curl. But still, I was torn. On the one hand, Aikins, MacAulay and Thorvaldson had been very generous to me and had given me my start. But Wellington West was making it easier to curl while still working. I decided that if I was really going to go all-in on curling, it made sense to make a move. I was very sad to leave, but life is all about growth and change, and I knew this was an important next step.

The team at Wellington West was a lot of fun. Any time I returned from a big event, like the Scotties or a world championship, my office would be full of balloons and there would be some sort of celebration. I felt like I was part of one big family. I remain grateful to Charlie and Blaine for their vision to bring me on board, and their trust and belief in me.

It took a while for me to establish my career, but once I did, I was proud that I'd been able to succeed while balancing two different, yet equally important, sides of my life.

4

A BIG PART OF A SMALL TEAM

WHEN OUR TEAM lost out on the chance to play at the world junior championship in that unusual playdown system, my junior curling days were over. The next season, 1995–96, I would start as a 21-year-old, and it meant a new team.

I was asked to play with Karen Fallis (later Porritt), who was a top skip in Manitoba and had won the 1981 Canadian junior championship. I was extremely flattered . . . and a bit taken aback. At that point, I loved the game and had success in juniors but never thought someone as high profile as Karen would reach out. I never gave myself a lot of credit and suffered from a lack of confidence. It was and remains my biggest hurdle to overcome. But I jumped at the opportunity. I played third, and Lynn Fallis-Kurz, Karen's sister, and Dana Allerton were on the front end.

After playing skip the previous few years, it was definitely a big change for me to throw third rocks and sweep a little more, but I knew I needed to experience the game at a higher level than juniors so I told myself to be a sponge, soak it up and learn as much as I could. Karen was a great mentor, and we had our

ROCK STAR

successes that year but didn't accomplish our goal of winning the province.

At that time, Manitoba had great depth, and it was exceptionally hard just to make it to the provincial championship—let alone win it. Curlers such as Connie Laliberte, Maureen Bonar and Cathy Overton-Clapham were the skips of the top teams. We'd play them in competitive events, and while we won a few games now and then, it was clear to me that we needed to get a lot better if we were going to get to the Canadian championship.

Our second year together produced pretty much the same results. We weren't disappointed in our play, but there was something lacking. That's when Karen came to me and suggested I take over as skip. She said we'd won some games but lost too many for us to feel satisfied. We were sort of treading water in the Manitoba curling scene, and we wanted to move forward. Karen thought this was the way to make some progress.

At first, I was shocked because she had enjoyed a lot of success skipping teams over her career. But I also knew that skip was where I wanted to play. The timing worked too. I had just graduated from law school, so I could devote more energy to curling. I agreed to the move and since that time, I've never played any other position.

I'm not sure if I was destined to be a skip, but that position has always felt natural to me. It's not that I needed to skip, but I enjoyed it more than the other positions. Part of the reason is just who I am. No matter what I'm doing—curling, working, making dinner—my mind is always planning and thinking, and so when I'm on the ice, I can turn that into a way to follow the game. I love the strategy of curling, and when I'm skipping, I'm

A BIG PART OF A SMALL TEAM

always thinking of the next shot and sometimes even two, three or four shots ahead. As many people say, curling is chess on ice. When I'm curling, I'm totally immersed in the game. I get completely lost in the moment, wondering what my opponent will do if we play a certain shot. I'm constantly trying to understand the other skip's calls and what my next move is going to be, and I love it. But the main reason I love skipping is the last shot. I know a lot of curlers who live in fear of having to throw the final stone with the game on the line. And I respect the fact that they know that about themselves.

Most of my teammates over the years were open about the fact they didn't want to skip. They wanted to be a part of a great team but understood their strengths and weaknesses. Most of us aren't willing to be vulnerable enough to admit when something scares us. But when you do it's freeing, and that's a big part of what made us so successful. We each played and owned our positions. For me, though, I love having the rock in my hands for the last shot. I love the adrenaline rush of the unknown. I love being the leader on my team and being able to be there when they need me the most. I absolutely love it. Having control of the situation makes me feel calm. There is nothing I enjoy more than being able to determine the outcome of a game. Understanding and accepting that about myself took some time, however.

In 2001, we made it to the Manitoba provincial championship and advanced all the way to the final. I missed a very important shot in a game against Karen Young, who would go on to win the title that year. There are very few shots that have stuck with me and caused me sleepless nights, but that was one of them. Mostly because I believe if I had made that shot, we likely would have won that game. I let my team down. After reflecting on it, I gradually changed my approach to those make-or-break moments in the game. Rather than playing down their importance, I learned to embrace how big those moments were. I would put 100 percent into those moments, ensuring that my focus was optimal, and when the game was over, I would have no regrets. It got to a point where I was so good at the big moments that I had to remind myself to focus for the simple shots.

My approach was the opposite of what every sports psychologist was telling us at the Curling Canada training camps. They would always say, "Pretend it is like practice." They tried to instill in us that we should treat every shot with the same approach, no matter whether it's the first rock of the game or the last to decide the winner. A draw to the four-foot is the same in the first end as it is in the 10th. But, for me, that's just not true—it was the opposite. Before every big shot, I'd take a breath and narrow my focus on what I had to do. It was important to understand the magnitude of the moment. The key to ensuring the best chance of success was to make sure I realized the importance of that particular shot. The bigger the shot, the more I was able to perform.

Some people live in fear of missing that last shot; I think about making it. I think about how good I am going to make it. It's not about what if I don't; it's what if I do. That's the way my mind works when I'm in the hack, about to throw the last stone of the end or the last stone of the game. As I reflect on my life and my earlier lack of confidence, I wish I'd embraced this mindset

A BIG PART OF A SMALL TEAM

sooner. To say to myself *Why not me?* instead of *Why me?* When I think like this, it allows me to believe that anything is possible.

I could not wrap my head around the entire pretend-it's-practice concept. Same ice, same rock, same thrower. Important games weren't just practice, and to treat them as such meant not understanding the feelings that arise and must be managed in those moments: the excitement bubbling up, the tingling of the nerves, the butterflies in your stomach. I didn't feel these things in practice, so when those feelings kicked in, it made me feel like I was failing in the big moments. *Why do I have butterflies? Why can't I control my nerves?* It wasn't authentic for me to believe it was practice because it wasn't. These feelings of excitement were why I played. I realized I loved the adrenaline rush of big moments. I was performing at the highest level of my sport and should leave it all on the ice. So I would sit in the hack, and in my mind I would tell myself, *Jennifer, this is a big shot. This is important. Don't screw this up.* It may not be a common approach, or what's advised in Sports Psychology 101, but it worked for me.

BEING AUTHENTIC TO yourself and understanding your emotions are pivotal, not just to curling, but to living a life full of joy. It's a life lesson that goes far beyond sports. I've passed this message on to others at my speaking engagements. Doing things differently from what you've been told doesn't mean what you're doing is wrong. However, in order to have this security and authenticity in your own approach, both in life and sport, you need to be surrounded by people who support you and will stand by you when things don't work out.

Of course, I never wanted to let my team down. Being there for my team in the big moments was one of the reasons I loved throwing the last stone. However, when I missed, I felt like I let them down. I carried this responsibility so deeply that it would impact me for days. I knew this wasn't healthy, and I needed to find a solution. After a lot of self-reflection, I had some uncomfortable conversations with my team. It wasn't my teammates who made the conversations uncomfortable—it was me. I was very anxious and didn't want to have any type of emotional conversation with other people. I preferred to deal with things internally.

My whole life, the happiness of those around me always took centre stage, and I never really thought about what I needed. When I would miss and let my team down, it hurt me to the core because the sport was the focus of my life. When I finally sat down and spoke to my teammates, I realized that all anyone was expecting of me was to try my best. Perfection wasn't the goal; it was all about effort. And that was all I wanted from the people around me too. For people to try their best and be accountable for their performance and actions. Why did I expect more of myself? Realizing this changed me personally and led to a lot of self-growth.

A weight I had been carrying for so long had been lifted. This need for perfection, which was impossible to attain, was gone. I felt free. I had finally opened the door to success and true happiness. I no longer felt like I was constantly failing and letting everyone down. This realization was also the big reason I never wanted to impose requirements on my teams. As part of our training, coaches at Curling Canada urged us to document

A BIG PART OF A SMALL TEAM

when we were going to practise and train and so many other details. They wanted us to create a record of our expectations. However, I believed this only led to more stress and pressure. In my opinion, competing successfully comes down to personal accountability and trust. If we didn't have these two integral parts in our team, we wouldn't be successful anyway. Personal accountability and trust became the secret sauce for our success.

As a result, whenever we had a new teammate, we worked on developing trust and the understanding and expectation that we would always have each other's backs, no matter what. It was vital that we trusted each other and that we could all accept the result, no matter what it might be. Whether it was my shot, a shot earlier in the end, a sweeping error or a bad line call, we all knew there were no other teammates we would rather have and that we were leaving it all out there for each other. This mindset was freeing and performance enhancing. Making sure to accept someone for who they are and what they bring was also important. It's easy to surround yourself with like-minded people who are similar to you, but that also means you might be missing out on a different perspective. Accepting our team-mates for who they were and what they brought to the team individually brought balance and perspective and was a core strength of every team I played on.

EVER SINCE I lost that Canadian junior final and sat and cried, I have come to understand that no one is trying to miss. Every player hopes to make the shot perfectly, but it won't always happen for a variety of reasons. Some of those reasons are outside of our control. That's what team sports are all about, and it is a privilege to be able to compete at the highest level, but with that comes uncertainty of the outcome. But isn't that why we play? If making the shot was a guarantee, why would we even curl? If we knew we were going to win every time, it wouldn't be very interesting or much fun. Fans would never tune in and the sport would fizzle. Some of the best games I've played have ended up as losses. It's the unknown that makes sport so exciting and worth the time and passion we put into trying to be the best.

One thing I have learned through all of the highs and lows is that whether it's a casual game at my club or for an Olympic gold medal, I'm only too happy to throw the last shot. That's just who I am.

There's one other reason why skipping appealed so much to me, and it may seem odd. I'm an introvert, an introvert in the biggest way. Many people are surprised by this as they see me as a person screaming on TV. But quiet is my peace and it always has been.

I was quite shy growing up, and I tried many sports. My dad loved sports, and his love was passed on to me. Because of my shy nature, making friends and being in big groups was challenging for me. However, when I was playing sports on a team, it was an easy first step, an entry into meeting new people. I tried everything. From baseball and volleyball to track. However, it was curling where I was most at home and comfortable. I found baseball was just a big team on which I felt lost, and track was individual, and I was alone. But curling was perfect. I was a big part of a small team. It was a dream come true.

A BIG PART OF A SMALL TEAM

To add to the perfection, when I was skipping, for most of the game I was on my own, standing at the opposite end to the rest of my team, and that made me feel more comfortable. I know this sounds unusual, but the opportunity to be by myself during the game was a significant part of my success. I could be in my own thoughts, be without distractions and noise, think on my own and plan out the strategy. It always energized me as it really fit with my comfort of being quiet and introspective, an introvert. It was like it was meant to be.

This doesn't mean I didn't like being with the other three players. In fact, I loved it, and I loved their input and the camaraderie. But when I was playing third, it always felt a bit crowded, which is just something that can be difficult for me. It was harder for me to clear my mind to a single train of thought. It was tiring instead of energizing.

When I took over as skip, I was still learning, game by game. Playing against some of the best women's teams in the world was very educational. At most bonspiels, we'd be facing off against top Manitoba teams such as Young, Lois Fowler and Barb Spencer, as well as rinks from other provinces like Alberta's Cathy Borst and Colleen Jones of Nova Scotia.

Karen, Lynn, Dana and I worked hard and really began to show that not only did we belong but we could beat anyone on any given day. After coming close in 2001, losing in the provincial final to Young, we finally broke through and won the Manitoba championship in 2002, defeating Linda Van Daele in the championship game (coincidentally enough, Jill Officer played on Linda Van Daele's team).

The competition was held at the Deer Lodge Curling Club

ROCK STAR

in Winnipeg, and for the final, the place was packed. Just about everyone I knew was in that club, watching the game. I had never felt more loved. All of my family, friends and colleagues came to cheer us on. It was a big deal!

It was a dream final. We came out firing and got off to an early lead and never looked back. Yes, having a game come down to the last shot is more exciting, but on the other hand having a commanding lead and being able to completely soak in the moment is incredible. Especially for the first win. I will never forget it and how excited everyone in the crowd was. It was a moment of a lifetime.

After we managed to leave the club, there was a gathering back at my house. When we walked in the door, there was a recording of bagpipes playing and a huge roar. I can remember just how happy everyone was for us. All my friends can remember that moment too. It was that big. A once-in-a-lifetime moment. It really was just the beginning, but back then I felt like it could be the only time we would ever feel this elation. It was a dream-come-true moment in every sense of the word.

My dad was almost more excited about us winning than we were, although he was still a bit shocked at what we'd accomplished.

"I knew you were good at curling," he said to me at the party, "but I didn't know you were going to make it to the Scotties." I will never forget the look in his eyes. I was living his dream and mine. He loved to curl but never got to play in the big games on centre stage. He was so proud and truly understood what this meant to me.

My mom was of course beyond proud and showed up wearing

A BIG PART OF A SMALL TEAM

her Manitoba "Jennifer Jones's Mom" jacket, which she brought to every single championship. She loves that jacket, and I smiled every time I saw it. Fans would spot it and even ask for her autograph.

Curling has always been big in Winnipeg, maybe more so than anywhere else in the world, and that meant we were big news now. Our win was on the front page of the *Winnipeg Free Press* and the *Winnipeg Sun* the following day. We were interviewed on the local television stations and on the radio by the legendary announcer Bob Picken. If he was interviewing you, it meant you'd done something special.

A few days later, I got an email from Robin Wilson, which was the moment everything became real. Wilson is a two-time Canadian champion who has been the director of the Scotties Tournament of Hearts since it started and a big reason the Scotties grew to what it is today. That letter was like our official entry. She congratulated our team and then began to tell us all the great things that were going to happen to us at the Canadian championship. It was our welcome-to-dreamland moment. The email really made it sink in that we were going to play in the Scotties.

We didn't have to travel far to play our first championship. That year's event was just over in Brandon at the Keystone Centre, where I'd watched my first Scotties. We also didn't have much time, with only a little over two weeks from the time we won the province to the start of the national final. There was a lot to pack into that short period.

For starters, because we were the host province team, I was asked to do some pre-tournament promotion. I went out about a week before the tournament and talked to the media, did some interviews and pumped up the event in Brandon to drive ticket sales. And, of course, we asked Jill Officer to join the team as alternate.

We also had to buy matching outfits—blazers and skirts—to wear at off-ice events like the opening banquet. To be honest, this was the most difficult thing about curling. Trying to find matching outfits in Manitoba colours—in two weeks—that fit everyone. And Dana was pregnant. But all of this felt like "the Show." The dream had come true. They have done away with this tradition, which is sad in some ways because it brought so much pride. But life is an evolution and it was time to move forward.

We also tried to keep up our practice, hoping we could ride the hot hand into a Canadian championship. And there was also the small matter of work, as we all still had full-time jobs.

Eventually the day came when we set off on Highway No. 1 for Brandon. I remember that the car ride felt as if we were floating, as if our energy and excitement were carrying us down the road. When we arrived, we found our hotel rooms done up with massive gift baskets from Scott Paper, filled with everything you could think of. There was also a gift from the host committee: a pair of slippers with the Scotties logo on them. The most beautiful slippers I had ever seen. I didn't want to wear them and ruin them. I decided they would be my Scotties slippers, and they were only worn at every Scotties I competed in. They lasted for over 20 years and were at my last Scotties. We no longer receive a gift from the host committee, which is understandable. However, I have kept these small treasures because

A BIG PART OF A SMALL TEAM

they are a symbol of the kindness of these incredible volunteers to make our dreams beyond our wildest expectations. It never went unnoticed.

After getting settled in, we decided to walk over to the arena, which was almost empty at that point, awaiting the arrival of the curlers and the fans. When we walked in, it brought chills, seeing the ice, the rocks all lined up, the boards with all the ads on them and the stands that would soon be filled. Aside from that, the icemakers were putting the final touches on the playing surface, but the only other people in the arena were a few security personnel. It was empty and quiet.

As all four of us looked around wide-eyed at what would be our home for the next week, the introvert in me took over. I left the others and walked up into the seats. I found a place about 12 rows up and sat down, looking out over the ice, which appeared so pristine, a perfect playing surface. I tried to guess on which of the four sheets of ice the championship game would be played. I imagined myself on the ice, throwing a rock as the crowd roared. I did my best to drink it all in and soak up the moment because I didn't know if this was going to be my only time at the Scotties. This moment of being alone in the peace and quiet became a tradition for me at all the future championships I played. You could always see me before the event started, closing my eyes and trying to imprint this memory into my soul forever. It was my way of realizing how grateful I was to have the opportunity and the ability to play in the greatest of championships. In that moment I always felt like I had won, no matter the outcome.

The opening draw was the complete opposite of that moment I had in the stands. We lined up in the tunnel underneath the

ROCK STAR

stands with a flag-bearer holding our provincial flag and a junior curler carrying the Manitoba sign. At the front of the line was a pipe band that was getting ready to lead us in. There was a lot of nervous anticipation, not only for our team but all of the curlers who were about to make their entrance. We laughed and smiled at each other, realizing it was about to happen.

When the pipes started up, the music just ran through my body. And as we made our entrance into the arena, I couldn't believe the fans who seemed to fill every part of the facility. Looking around, it was hard to comprehend that all these people were coming to watch us play.

I've made that march into the rink hundreds of times since that first one, and it's something that never gets old. The chills went down my spine on that day just as they have every time since. To me it means we're about to start playing but also that everyone in that arena, player or fan, is about to celebrate this great game.

As the week went on, we became more comfortable with the surroundings, and our game shined. We ended up with an 8-3 record that had us in a three-way tie for second. That put us into the 3-versus-4 sudden-death playoff game against Ontario's Sherry Middaugh, which we lost. As rookies, I thought we played well, and more than that, I felt we all enjoyed the experience.

So many moments that week have stayed with me over my career. Several represented just the start of long-lasting relationships. For instance, that Scotties was where I first encountered Jim Young, a cameraman for TSN. Many of our games were televised that year, and Jim was one of the cameramen who always seemed to be there, shooting the close-ups of us as we threw our rocks. Outside of the curlers and officials, the television crew spends the most time inside the boards. When you see them at event after event, year after year, you get to know them. They become your friends and part of the curling family.

Jim and I became fast friends and kept in touch outside of curling championships. Years later, at the Scotties in Regina, we were checking into the hotel at the same time. I went to give him a hug and noticed he appeared to be on the verge of tears. I asked him if everything was OK.

"My father just called me to say he has terminal cancer," he replied. "He only has a short time left."

Jim had told me many times that his father was a big fan of mine, so I told him to call his father and give me the phone. I chatted with his dad for about half an hour, doing what I could to try to lift his—and Jim's—spirits. Considering the circumstances, it wasn't much, but his father seemed overjoyed to think that I would call him. When the call ended, I could see the smile on Jim's face. That's the kind of friendship we had, and it all started at that first Scotties. He was my friend, my family. He was there through my highs and lows with the biggest hugs. No words were needed. He knew. I am so grateful our paths crossed. Jim taught me to always live life to the fullest and to be grateful for the great people in our lives. That genuine kindness will never be forgotten.

Sadly, in 2022, Jim also passed away from cancer, and I was grateful I saw him a few days before to say goodbye. He told me to keep being me because I was special, to hug my girls, to never stop smiling, and that things aren't important . . . moments and memories are. That was Jim and I miss him terribly.

ROCK STAR

As we left Brandon there were two thoughts: The first was that I was thrilled at having made it to the Scotties and that we played well in the championship. No one could take that away from us. The second was that I wanted more. I wanted to come back and play again. And I wanted to win. I always thought if I could just play in one Scotties, my dreams would be fulfilled.

Once you've played in the Canadian championship, you get hooked. It is such an amazing event that it makes all the hard work, the early-morning on-ice practice sessions, the late-night training at the gym and the sacrifices on the social calendar worth it. It was beyond my wildest dreams.

The following year our team played well, but we couldn't defend our Manitoba title and so there was no return trip to the Scotties.

Not only that, it became increasingly clear that the four of us had done all we could together. We'd played well and we'd enjoyed the run, but we were all headed in different directions in our lives. By their own admission, Karen and Lynn both had young kids at home and full-time jobs that made it difficult to devote as much time as necessary to remain at the top of their games.

We met and talked about what we'd accomplished and what the next steps would be. When the season ended, so did that team. There was no animosity; rather, we were proud of our accomplishments and our friendship. We remain friends to this day, and I am grateful for their support and friendship.

For me personally, the past was something to cherish, and the future promised to be even more exciting.

5

WHY NOT ME?

NOT LONG AFTER our team decided to go our separate ways, I found myself with Cathy Gauthier. A seasoned curler, Cathy had played much of her career with the great Connie Laliberte, winning Canadian championships in 1992 and '95. It was great to call her a friend and be able to spend time with her and observe the dedication that she and her team had put in to reach the success they were justifiably enjoying. Cathy knew I was a free agent. When a team breaks up, the news spreads like wildfire. The breakup was so recent that Cathy likely guessed I hadn't yet decided what I was going to do the following season.

Out of the blue, she threw a question my way: "Would you ever consider playing with Cathy Overton-Clapham?"

The question wasn't meant as anything more than casual conversation—at least that was my impression. Still, I was taken aback by how sudden it seemed—and at the name she tossed out. Cathy Overton-Clapham was one of the best curlers in the province and had been on the 1995 Manitoba team with Gauthier and Laliberte that won the Canadian championship. She'd skipped

ROCK STAR

a Manitoba team to the Canadian junior title in 1989. By the time Gauthier asked me the question, Overton-Clapham had already made five trips to the Scotties.

I had a hard time comprehending what Gauthier was asking me. Was Overton-Clapham really interested in curling with me? Or was this simply some pie-in-the-sky dream? No way would someone this good want me to join up on a team with them.

But Gauthier was playing matchmaker. She had yet to talk with Overton-Clapham, whose team had recently broken up. But she was trying to bring the two of us together. I was her first stop on this mission.

It took me a few seconds to process Cathy Gauthier's question, but then my answer came quickly: "Yes!" I wasn't even particular about the position I'd play. Third or skip, it didn't really matter as long as I was going to be on what could be a powerhouse squad.

With my answer in her pocket, Gauthier set out to see if Overton-Clapham would agree. She didn't waste time, immediately getting on the phone.

The response was equally swift and enthusiastic. Overton-Clapham was on board—more than excited to join forces and see where we could go.

The rest of the team came together quite easily. Jill Officer was back in Winnipeg after attending school in Brandon. She'd been the fifth player on my team that went to the Scotties in 2002. I always felt that when Jill finished school, we'd somehow curl together.

The final position was filled by none other than Cathy Gauthier. She never told me if this was part of the plan all along, but after connecting Overton-Clapham and me, she wasn't going to miss out on joining what we all felt was going to be a dynamic team.

As for positions, Overton-Clapham suggested that I skip. She had played third for some years and enjoyed the position. And she was one of the best thirds ever to play, so it seemed a good fit. I was happy to remain at skip because I felt that's where I played best. Jill stepped in at second. And though Cathy Gauthier took over at lead, that was a new spot for her; in fact, she'd never played lead before. But she was gung-ho to be on this team, and if it meant learning to play lead, she was only too happy to do so.

So in the course of about three days, thanks to Cathy Gauthier's simple question, I went from not knowing what the next curling season was going to look like to joining a squad that had the potential to go a long way.

Right from the first time we got together, I could see this was going to be a different team. It was a squad built to enjoy our time together, but more than anything, all four of us wanted to win. And to do that, we were all prepared to do whatever it took.

Along with all this excitement, I felt great pressure on us to succeed. We were about the highest-profile team in the province, and with that came plenty of expectations. We weren't front-page news—yet—but already the word was out about us and how we were going to be one of the favourites, not only to win the province but possibly to contend for the Canadian title.

For me, it was about making a huge commitment to the team and also realizing I was still practising law; as always, finding the time to do everything was going to be tough. There were lots of pensive moments in the early days when I wondered how I was going to be able to do it all and still find time to sleep.

One of the first things we did as a team was sign on Cal Botterill, one of the top sports psychologists in the country. In his younger days, Cal had been a top hockey player and a part of the Canadian national hockey team from 1967 to '69. Later, he earned a PhD in psychology, focusing on sports performance. Overton-Clapham had worked with him in the past, and she was adamant that our new lineup should retain Cal.

The first time we met with Cal was at his cottage in West Hawk Lake, which sits right on the Manitoba-Ontario border. The isolation of that spot let us focus on our work. Appropriately named Serenity, the cottage became a serene escape. Cal invited us out to the cottage whenever he felt we needed to pause from everything that was going on. For the first time in my life, I thought about mental well-being as something I should consider. Cal opened my eyes to rest and recovery. Before I worked with him, I thought I could do it all and that recovery and rest were a waste of my valuable time. Serenity would become my favourite place in the world.

Although I was interested to see what sports psychology could do for our team, I felt uncomfortable going into our first meeting. Talking about my feelings is not something I like doing. In fact, it's my worst nightmare. Here I was about to share my thoughts not only with Cal but with my new teammates as well.

Yet right from that initial meeting, I could tell that Cal was going to become an integral part of our new team. Perhaps even more importantly, I could see he was going to have a huge impact on me as a curler and as a person. He made me feel comfortable from the start. Once I was at ease, it became easier to open up.

One of the first things Cal asked us all to do was take a personality test, a common opening step for sports psychologists to take. He wanted to know a little more about us. I asked him if I should answer the questions as if I was Jennifer Jones, the curler, or Jennifer Jones, the person away from curling.

"Well, Jennifer," he answered with a smile. "There really shouldn't be a difference between those two people."

We chuckled about that comment, but the test was the starting point for how Cal really changed me. He could see that our team needed a leader; as the skip, that should be my role. I always felt differently. For me, every player on the team should be equal. That's how I'd worked with my previous teams. We all had our positions, but the sum of the parts is what made it all click.

Cal didn't disagree with me about the equality idea, but he told me that someone has to make the final decision—and that was me. He said I needed to exude confidence and to inspire greatness from everybody. The players would feed off me just by the nature of the lineup and the responsibilities.

At first, I wasn't sure I could do what Cal wanted. It wasn't something that came to me naturally. Throughout my career I'd been more of a pleaser. I wanted to make everyone happy and not ruffle any feathers. If I made the final decision and it went against someone else's idea, I was sure I would piss off someone on the team. It would weigh on me for days.

ROCK STAR

Cal helped me understand why it was important that I become the leader and what it would mean for us. As we worked over the summer, he helped me accept the role that my teammates needed from me. They were expecting it, he told me. And in our group sessions, the team would confirm that feeling.

It wasn't an easy transition for me. I had to push myself into doing something that at first made me slightly uncomfortable. Part of the difficulty was that I was now on a team where everyone had already experienced so much success. I was intimidated by what they had done and a bit worried that I wouldn't measure up.

Cal helped me overcome my uncertainties with one three-word question: Why not me?

Why not me? That really resonated. Up to that point, I saw a world full of people who looked at things negatively and focused more on what could go wrong than on what could go right. I never thought there was something special about me. I loved to curl, but I wasn't special.

Why can't I win? Cal would ask me to ask myself. *Why can't it be me on the top step of the podium? Why can't I be successful? Why can't I overcome this challenge?*

It's not an overstatement to say these conversations changed my curling career. They became the mantra I would fall back on when I lost confidence. I had enjoyed success on the ice and yet, up to that point, I really lacked confidence in almost every game I played.

Cal's approach gave me a new outlook. It was not unlike something the great quarterback Tom Brady said at a celebration of his retirement from the NFL: "To be successful at anything,

WHY NOT ME?

the truth is you don't have to be special. You just have to be what most people aren't: consistent, determined and willing to work for it."

Why not me? is something that's stayed with me my entire career. It's been a way of thinking that has carried me through tough games, the championships, the off-season training and even life moments outside of curling. Because that phrase is so powerful, I've talked about it in my home and with my family. Instead of focusing on the bad things, blaming someone or something else or wanting a pity party because of a situation, it's important to look at the positives and what might happen. This life lesson obviously resonated because, years later, one of my daughters wrote a short story for a school project that she titled "Why Not Me?" I shed a tear. At 10 years of age, she realized the value of asking herself this question. It took me a lot longer to grasp its significance.

There was a lot more to the work we did with Cal that summer, and all of his efforts helped bring our team together. Considering we hadn't yet played a game, that was quite re-markable. A bit of a mixed bag, we were all at different points in our lives. The two Cathys were each married and had kids, Jill was fresh out of college and I was in the early stages of my career as a lawyer.

Cal helped us put everything on the table, explaining what we were all capable of committing to. He also got us to buy into goals as a team and be sure we were pulling together. Our goals were lofty but realistic. We wanted to win the Cana-dian championship. Once we all agreed on that, we spent time building a pathway to getting there.

ROCK STAR

The driving force behind all this work with Cal was Overton-Clapham. She was big on the psychology of sport, and it showed in how talented and driven she was. From the first time I met her, I could see she had a winning quality as well as a tremendous work ethic. On or off the ice, in or out of the gym, she was driven. She had grit and determination, and nothing was going to be left to chance. No matter what the score or the circumstances, she was going to find a way to win.

She wasn't shy about having this attitude, and it really rubbed off on us.

In addition to working with Cal, our team adopted a rigorous training schedule, both on and off the ice. My previous team had practised but not like what we were doing with this new rink. It was hard work and took a big commitment, but I simply loved the environment I was now part of. I knew we had what it would take to win the Canadian championship and to be the best. I was willing to make sacrifices to reach our goal, and—the best part—my teammates were too.

By the time the season started, we were as prepared as any team—and it showed. We enjoyed a solid season of cashspiels, though at that time there weren't many of them for women. We advanced to the provincial playdowns, which were back at the St. Vital Curling Club where I'd won my first Manitoba title, and we were seeded No. 1 in the draw. We played well that week and came out on the right side of a number of tough games, eventually claiming the Manitoba title.

We were excited with the win, and as with my first title, there was another celebration. It was great to be going back to the Scotties. But this one felt different. Now it was as if winning

WHY NOT ME?

the provincial title was the first step toward our overall goal. There was certainly nothing wrong with being Manitoba champions and getting to wear the Buffalo crest on our sweaters. But after all the hard work and the grinding season, we were after bigger things.

The national championship that year was in St. John's, Newfoundland and Labrador, and the people there couldn't have been nicer and more welcoming. From the moment our plane touched down, we felt like rock stars on the Rock. The local committee had done a tremendous job preparing for the event, and a large group of volunteers did everything from selling tickets to cleaning the ice.

At that time, at all the national championships, each team would get its own volunteer driver to chauffeur them around for the week. (Now we're given a rental car, which is nice but you don't make the same lifetime connections.) Most often, the trip would be from the hotel to the rink and back, but there might be side trips as well, such as out for dinner or perhaps a shopping excursion. Because we spent so much time in the van, the drivers often became good friends with the team, leading to long-lasting relationships.

That was the case that year with our driver, Karen Harvey, who immediately became a member of the team for that week. But there was one unusual part about her job: The hotel we stayed in was attached to the arena, so we didn't need a drive to get there. We simply took the elevator from our rooms and walked through the lobby and a couple of doors, and there we were.

Still, Karen did her job dutifully. Every morning, she'd meet

ROCK STAR

us in the lobby and walk us over and then repeat the task in the opposite direction after our games, dropping us back at the elevator. Within moments of meeting her, I knew that Karen would forever be family. Karen was a person who glowed. She taught me the importance of kindness and hospitality. She made us feel special and welcome. She is the kind of person that all human beings should strive to become. It was East Coast hospitality on steroids.

When we would go on the ice, Karen would sit up in the stands with our families, becoming part of our support squad. As the week went on, she and my parents grew close. (So close, in fact, that in later years, my folks took a trip to Newfoundland and visited Karen and her incredible husband, Paul, in St. John's.) Whenever we played in Newfoundland, my family—including my daughters—had a place to stay. We were always welcomed with open arms. "Poppi Paul," as our girls called Karen's husband, was always there for story time. We lost Paul to cancer way too young, and it makes me grateful that our paths crossed. He will forever be part of our family, and his memory will live on. Paul was one of a kind, and the world was a much better place with him in it. We're planning more visits to Newfoundland, where I know we'll create new memories to cherish.

A close friend and one of my favourite people in the world, Karen is often the first person to message me when something happens, good or bad, curling or otherwise.

That same week in Newfoundland, we met Mark Britt. Mark worked for Fairmont, the hotel chain, and was a huge curling fan. He was at the championship as a guest of Scotties' parent

WHY NOT ME?

company, Kruger. It was his first time at a national championship, and he had a blast. Mark was at the banquet held after the round robin and came by to ask for a picture. He told us he'd placed a friendly wager on us to win. He won that bet and continued making his friendly wager for years to come.

Mark would show up at a number of Scotties over the years, and we'd always find time to chat. Even away from the Scotties, our team would correspond with him or he would come to watch us play if we were in an event close to his home in Ontario.

We became so close, in fact, that when he celebrated his 50th birthday, his friends from his curling club got me to fly into Burlington, Ontario, as a surprise, and I even played a curling game with him. Covid brought an end to Mark's attendance streak, but he flew on his own and surprised me at my final Scotties. He had been there for all of them, and he wanted to be at this one to support me as I said goodbye. That is what curling is. Karen and Mark are examples of why curlers and curling are so great. The friendships and relationships that start at a club or an event can last a lifetime. I often talk about how small acts of kindness have changed my life and curling career. Karen and Mark exemplify the big impact that small acts of kindness can make. I will always talk about the game's evolution and the need to embrace change—that's a part of life. Yes, the championships have changed over the years. We're often left on our own, and the teams must seek out these human connections. Trust me when I say it is so worth talking to the volunteers. Their stories and the friendships you can make will change your life.

In St. John's, our hotel room was full of gifts from the

sponsor and the volunteers—as it had been at my last Scotties. I had remembered to bring my Scotties slippers from the last national championship, and I wore them proudly around the room. In those years, we were grateful for the opportunity to compete on this incredible stage and never challenged anything. In the early days, the competitors all walked to church for service on Sunday. That was before my time, but everyone went without question. It was a different era and would never happen in today's world.

There were, however, certain aspects of the competition that were hard to wrap my head around. We were told by the event managers what uniforms to wear—from our pants to our jackets to how our shirts were to be tucked in—and that we could never look "sloppy." We were creating an image. I understood the concept, but at the same time I didn't understand why we couldn't be ourselves. I wanted to grow women's curling as much as anyone, but why did we need to look a certain way to sell our product? Could we not just shine in our talent and what we did on the ice?

We had to wear brand new polyester pants that caused rashes and chafed our inner thighs. By the middle of the week, we were raw! (Maybe this is why my mom wore pantyhose under those awful pants.) We had to go to the drugstore to try to find creams for relief, but there was also drug testing and banned substances—so we needed to be careful. To make matters worse, the pants were so baggy—they looked like something MC Hammer would have worn in a 1990 video—they would drag on the ice, affecting our feel for draw weight. They made it

WHY NOT ME?

more difficult to curl. Our shirts had to be tucked, but the pants were ridiculously high-waisted. If you can't imagine the look, just google the 2005 Scotties final.

Meanwhile, our female parts were almost resting on the waistline for everyone to see. I tried to wear a long-sleeved shirt under my playing jersey, but I was told to change immediately because I looked sloppy. Never in my life had I been told I was sloppy. It made me feel terribly insecure about myself, which was not the best mindset for competing. But remember, this was 2005. At the time we were so grateful for the opportunity, we would have done anything. And the pants had the Scotties logo on them, making them feel special. I couldn't bear to throw them out, and they're in a bin somewhere in my basement. (But everything is relative. Pants from previous years were see-through to the point you could see the color of underwear the women were wearing.) When watching replays of the 2005 Scotties, our daughters will ask me why we wore those pants. I always say because "we had to." And the girls respond, "That is silly. Why?" Those were the rules then, and we had to comply. But we advocated for change, and change takes time.

We put the uniforms to the back of our minds and tried to concentrate on curling. On the ice, the team's strong play continued. We won six of our first seven games, defeating the legend Colleen Jones and her team, who were playing as Team Canada that year. That foursome had won the previous four national championships and five of the last six. Earning that win against one of the best teams of all time was a big achievement.

Our first loss came at the hands of my former teammate,

ROCK STAR

Kelly Scott from British Columbia, and we lost a second match to Prince Edward Island. But our 9-2 record allowed us to finish in top spot.

In our first playoff game, we managed to defeat Scott, and that win moved us into the final where we took on Ontario's Jenn Hanna.

We didn't come out strong in that match. In fact, we were down 4–2 after five ends and struggling to find our game. I was particularly off that day and couldn't seem to find my groove. I wasn't sure if it was the rocks or the ice or just me having a bad game, but I wasn't playing like I had in all the matches that got us to this point.

At the fifth-end break, I came down the ice to meet my three teammates, and I just pleaded with them to hang on.

"Look," I told them. "I know I'm not playing very well. But just stay with me. We can still win this. Just give me a shot to win and I promise we can make it." I looked them in the eyes so they could see I was with them.

Although I was speaking to Cathy, Jill and Cathy, I was probably talking to myself more than anyone. It was all part of that mental training Cal Botterill had instilled in me at the start of the season.

"You have to instill confidence," he would tell me. "You have to look at people in the eyes. You need to have your head held high, no matter what's going on." Those lessons came back to me at that moment. I was the leader on our team, and I needed to be the leader in that moment. Even when it was a struggle, I had to be there for my team. It was my role, my obligation and what I had agreed to do. And I wasn't going to let them down.

WHY NOT ME?

We rallied and scored single points in the seventh and eighth ends to narrow the score to 5–4, but then gave up a single point in the ninth end to fall behind by two heading to the final end.

That final end is one that I, my teammates and the curling world will never forget.

6

THE SHOT HEARD
ROUND THE WORLD

THERE HAVE BEEN a lot of famous curling shots in the history of the game. I immediately think of Northern Ontario's Al Hackner making a very thin double against Pat Ryan of Alberta in the 1995 Brier. Or Ontario's Glenn Howard making a long, complicated raise double against Joel Jordison of Saskatchewan at the 2009 Brier. (I'm particularly fond of this second one because my husband, Brent Laing, was on that team!)

In women's curling, Sandra Schmirler made a dramatic shot in the seventh end of the 1997 Olympic trials. She hit one of her own stones sitting well off on the side of the sheet and redirected the shooter into the centre of the house to remove the shot rock belonging to Shannon Kleibrink. That allowed Schmirler to score three, and two ends later, her team won and was off to the Olympics.

My most famous shot, and what many have told me could be curling's greatest, took place in the final end of that 2005 Scotties Tournament of Hearts against Ontario's Jenn Hanna.

ROCK STAR

What follows is a shot-by-shot description of how this end developed and how it led to what is now simply called "the Shot." (I realize some of the details may be complicated. You can find the last end on YouTube and follow along.)

The 10th end started with us trailing by two points but with last rock advantage. I was thinking our strategy was to try to score two, tie the game up and then take our chances in an extra end. The opportunity for three or more points wasn't out of the question, but at this level, and against a team such as Hanna's, that would be difficult.

At the start of the end, our job was to get as many rocks in play as possible. That would make it easier to score multiple points. Hanna wanted the opposite: to keep it as clean and open as she and her team could. Ontario's first rock, thrown by Steph Hanna, Jenn's sister, slid perfectly into the rings, sitting in the four-foot. Cathy Gauthier countered with a perfect corner guard.

On the second shot, Jenn Hanna asked her sister to throw the stone through the rings, just not wanting it in play to possibly crowd everything up. We countered by putting up a second corner guard on the opposite side of the sheet.

This opening was predictable and not unlike a standard opening in chess. They go in, we go guard; they throw it through, and we put up another guard. So far, neither team had any advantage. They knew what we were trying to do, and we knew their game plan.

Next up for Ontario was the second, Dawn Askin. In future years, she would join forces with me on a long and successful run (more on that in later chapters). But at that moment, she

THE SHOT HEARD ROUND THE WORLD

was trying to remove one of the guards sitting in front of the house.

Right out of her hand, there was a call for sweeping as the rock curled closer and closer to the guard. It made contact and our rock went out the back. But instead of rolling out, her shooter rolled slowly across the top of the house, coming to rest outside the rings—about six inches from the side board.

When it stopped, I immediately thought to myself, *We're going to need to use that rock*. It was still very early in the end, but where that rock was sitting and the angles that it provided were juicy. I knew I had to protect that stone and make sure that, if we needed to use it, we could.

Jill then replaced the corner guard, and the Ontario team immediately called for Dawn to remove it. This time there was no sweeping, but her shot hit the guard we had just thrown and rolled across the sheet, nudging our other guard into the rings and then rolling out of play. At that moment, it didn't seem like much. They had one in the four-foot and the other one out in the wings. We had one biting the 12-foot just off to one side of centre. I hadn't given up hope, but we needed to find a way to score at least two.

With her second shot of the end, Jill threw a guard on our stone. Ontario's third, Pascale Letendre, attempted to remove the guard but hit it on the nose and pushed our rock back onto our other one in the house, just clipping it. It slid over in front of their yellow one sitting near the centre of the rings.

Now things were starting to look good for us to score two. I asked Cathy Overton-Clapham to throw her shot so it would just bump their shot rock back about four or five feet. She threw

ROCK STAR

it well but moved it only about a foot. It was still shot rock, but not for long. Letendre tried to take it out but was wide. Her rock jammed our red onto their yellow, and we were now sitting first and third shot. The yellow stone that was second was wide open, and Cathy could leave us sitting three with a takeout.

That miss from Letendre was a huge momentum shift in our favour. It appeared as if we now had a chance not just to tie the game but to win it. Cathy came down to talk about her next shot just to make sure we were both certain about what I wanted her to do. We were sensing the importance of it and that this shot could make or break the game. We agreed on the shot and the weight, and as Cathy headed back to the hack, she quipped that she hadn't thrown a hit all game. Now I was asking her to throw one of the biggest of her career. It was a chance for us to sit three and give us a legitimate shot at scoring three and winning the Scotties.

Her throw was narrow out of her hand, and despite some furious sweeping, it jammed their yellow back onto our red, returning the favour they had just given us. Perhaps the only saving grace was that it was so light it didn't push our red stone out of the rings.

The emotional swings of those two shots were immense. At one moment, I thought we were going to score three and win. The next, it seemed as if we'd lost all hope. But the four of us didn't give up. I was proud of the fact that at that moment, we stayed patient and remained calm.

We didn't lose our cool in any way. Rather, we remained in the moment and began sizing up the possibilities.

As I looked over the house and tried to think of our next

THE SHOT HEARD ROUND THE WORLD

shot, I kept eyeing that yellow rock sitting well out in the wings. It was still very much in play and could end up being our saving grace.

With skip rocks remaining, they were sitting shot with a stone in the four-foot. We were second, third and fourth. On Jenn's first shot, their side called for a freeze on our stone that was second shot. That freeze would accomplish two things: guard their shot rock and also sit third, cancelling out the rocks we had at the side and back of the rings.

The shot came up short of the rings but still provided coverage for the shot stone, which was now tucked behind two long guards. I knew our main objective was to find a way to somehow get rid of that shot stone. The call was for a difficult shot: hit their long guard—driving it back onto our stone, which would then hit their shot stone. A double-raise takeout. If I missed, I was hoping I could still remove both their guards.

When I got down to the hack to play my shot, I wasn't nervous or anxious. I knew the shot I needed to play, and I set myself up for that. When I let it go, I thought it would be OK. In fact, both Cathy and I called the sweepers off. Then all at once it curled, hitting their long guard almost on the nose. There was no double-raise takeout. There was no removal of the guards. At that moment, with each of us having just one shot remaining, we were in a tough situation.

All I could do was look at that rock out in the wings.

I was a little surprised when Jenn elected to throw a guard with her last one. It was a safe call. But if she had come into the rings and played a freeze on our top stone or even a draw, she could have sat for second or third shot and made it impossible

ROCK STAR

for us to score more than two. When she headed down the ice to throw her shot, I felt a sense of relief that, at the very least, we were going to have a chance, a shot to win. How much more could we ask for?

When her guard came to rest, we immediately knew what we were going to do. We'd talked it over as she was playing her shot, and we were decisive in our call. That was good for obvious reasons, but also for the fact that our time clock was running down. We had less than two minutes to throw our rock, which meant there wasn't any time to discuss other options. Cathy Overton-Clapham and I went to the rock out at the side of the sheet and tried to find the perfect angle that would re-direct our stone onto the shot rock. As it turned out, there was a sticker on the handle of the stone. It indicated the rock number and was the perfect alignment aid.

"Just hit it right on the two," Cathy said.

This wasn't going to be an easy shot. In fact, it was probably the most difficult shot I'd ever thrown. On the broadcast, commentator Mike Harris concurred: "If she makes this shot, it will be the best shot I've ever seen."

The shot required me to throw it quite hard—and back then, not many women threw rocks at such great velocity. (Today, almost every top team does.) But to maintain enough speed after hitting the rock in the wings to still have enough force to remove the shot stone, I was going to have to reach back to fire it. And I still had to be on target.

Cathy and I decided on the line, and I turned to slide back down the ice. I can remember the murmuring of the fans as I

THE SHOT HEARD ROUND THE WORLD

made my way to the hack. The crowd buzzed with excitement as they sensed the shot I was attempting—it was electric.

As I approached the hack, I tried to visualize the shot and prepare myself for what I needed to do. I looked over at Jill and I thought she looked nervous. (She later told me she was scared she was going to trip on the boards and burn the rock.) Cathy Gauthier looked calm, although who knows what was going through her mind. There was some brief chit-chat about the weight, with both Jill and Cathy trying to sound as if it was the last shot in the first end of a club game—not one to win a national championship.

As I reached the end of the sheet, I tried to swallow but my mouth was as dry as the Sahara Desert. My heart was beating a million times a minute, pumping so hard I was sure it would pop out of my chest.

But in that moment, I realized this was my dream come true. I was standing in front of a packed arena—with hundreds of thousands more people watching on TV—with a shot at winning the Scotties. Yes, it was a very difficult shot. But it was what I'd always wanted and what I'd worked so hard for. Those training sessions, the practices and the games throughout the season had led me to this moment.

I still remember the smell of the building and the buzzing of the crowd. When I sat in the hack and flipped my rock over to clean it, the building went silent. It was eerie how quiet such a large group of people could be.

I made another attempt to swallow, but there was still nothing there. I made up my mind to enjoy this moment, took

ROCK STAR

a deep breath and realized that make it or not, I was exactly where I wanted to be. Then I told myself, as I do before any big shot, *Here goes nothing.*

I went into my delivery, driving out of the hack. As I let the rock go, I thought it was just the way I wanted to throw it. It had plenty of weight and was right on line. There was a brief pause, and then Cathy Overton-Clapham and I both screamed simultaneously for the sweepers. Cathy Gauthier and Jill were scrubbing as hard as they could. I saw Cathy look up at one point and then just find another gear as she swept as hard as humanly possible. She knew it was close. Jill was on the other side of the stone, furiously sweeping. At the hog line I yelled, "Whoa!" and all four of us just waited that split second to see if we'd hit the other rock perfectly and if it had enough power to remove it from the rings.

It took only seconds from the time the rock left my hand until the moment it pushed the Ontario stone from the rings, but it seemed like time was moving in slow motion. A second later, when the rocks all came to rest and we had scored four, the arena exploded. Someone told me later that the decibel level reached more than 100, which is equivalent to standing next to a jet engine on takeoff. I could feel the cheers in my bones. I thought my whole body was going to explode. I've never felt a rush of adrenaline like that again.

I was jumping up and down in celebration, and although it wasn't planned, I found myself standing right on the Scotties logo in the middle of the ice. (How's that for product placement?) After my first few initial screams, I looked down the ice and saw our alternate player, Trisha Eck, running toward me like

THE SHOT HEARD ROUND THE WORLD

a linebacker in a football game. Trisha is a very special friend. It meant the world that she was a part of this moment. Jill reached me first and we hugged. A moment later, the five of us were in a group hug, jumping up and down and still screaming.

After that broke up, I saw my father standing there. He'd served as our coach all week, and when I saw him, I almost lost it. We hugged like we'd never hugged before, and he just said, "Wow! What a shot, kid."

What a shot, indeed. It was a moment that every athlete wants. The perfect way to win not only a game but a championship.

After those initial moments of celebration, we managed to calm ourselves enough to head down the ice and shake hands with the Ontario foursome. It was easy to tell they were crushed, but they were more than gracious and respectful in congratulating us. Although we didn't know it at the time, Dawn Askin (later McEwen), whose rock we used to bounce our winning shot off, would be a member of our team in the coming years, and we'd have plenty of great moments together. I remember shaking her hand and seeing her smile at me. I'm sure that wasn't easy to do, considering the circumstances.

Somewhat lost in all the madness going on was the fact we were now Canadian champions. For the two Cathys, it was Canadian champions again. For Jill and me, it was a first. We were so busy celebrating the ending of the game that it took a moment to realize we were about to be presented with the championship trophy.

Closing ceremonies always take place almost immediately after the last rock has been played. There's a rush to present

ROCK STAR

the trophy on the television broadcast and also before people begin to leave the arena. So in the middle of our celebration, I had an official come over and help me get my jacket on because we needed to be in our full uniform for the closing. No matter how much sweat, you've got to look your best.

A few moments later, we were standing on the top step of the podium, being congratulated by several officials. Then we were invited to step down and walk over to the trophy, which was a little too heavy and awkward to lift. We gathered around it for the photographers to snap away. At one point, I could stand it no longer and I leaned over and kissed the trophy. I just wanted to make sure it was real!

The feeling of being the Canadian champion is hard for me to put into words. Though it's something I dreamed of, I never really knew if my dreams would come true. But I never stopped chasing my dreams because I think dreaming is part of living to the fullest. I remember thinking, after I kissed the trophy, *This is actually real. This is happening. This isn't a dream.* And in that moment, I honestly thought my life could not get any better.

As the years have elapsed since I threw that shot, it's never faded from my memory—or, apparently, from the memories of curling fans. It's rare that a week goes by without someone asking me about it or telling me where they were when it happened. Every February, when the Scotties are on the air, the shot gets some replays. Memories are refreshed, and the questions and chatter start again.

It's interesting that many curlers who didn't play the sport back when that shot happened now ask me about it. Because it's preserved on YouTube, people can see it with just the click of a

THE SHOT HEARD ROUND THE WORLD

mouse. The four of us—me, Cathy Overton-Clapham, Jill Officer and Cathy Gauthier—will be remembered forever in curling for that shot and the teamwork it took to make it happen.

That's a pretty overwhelming thought. When I started curling, I did it for the love of the game. I never considered I'd make a shot that would be regarded by many as the greatest in the sport's history.

That might sound boastful, but in 2019, TSN polled curlers and members of the curling media, asking them to rank the greatest shots of all time. Ours came out on top. When TSN aired the countdown of the best shots, there we were at No. 1, jumping up and down in our baggy pants. Our wardrobe might be the only part of that historic moment that I'd love to forget!

If there is a letdown that comes with winning the championship, it occurs after the trophy presentation. I thought we'd be celebrating with our families, drinking champagne and admiring our medals. Instead, we were immediately brought into a meeting room, where a lot of boring stuff unfolded. Over the years, I would understand that this was standard protocol. But after winning a national championship, it was like having the air let out of our tires.

First, two players from each team in the final are usually sent off to provide a sample for doping control, while the rest sit with Curling Canada officials. That testing process can take a while because it's not easy to pee in a bottle in front of the doping control officer. It's also common courtesy for the winners to let the losers go first.

We spent the next two hours going through everything from logistics of transportation to the world championship, to being measured for uniforms, to what our training would look like over the next couple of weeks. We had to sign athlete releases and other documents, mostly saying we'd be good Canadians and not break any rules.

Curling Canada was nice enough to have a bottle of wine for us, but at this point we didn't want to sip red and talk about jacket sizes. We wanted to spray champagne and hug our families. It dragged on and on and was a real case of lunch-bag letdown. (Thankfully, rules have changed over the years to allow some time with your family before drug testing and paperwork.)

On another occasion when we won, in 2015 in Moose Jaw, the meetings took so long that when we got out, all the volunteer drivers had left. That's understandable, of course, seeing they all had long weeks too. But we were left without a ride in a location that didn't have any Ubers and where the taxis had all shut down for the evening. There was no other way for us to get back to the hotel. Luckily, I found my friend Jim Young and some of his TSN colleagues. They'd just finished tearing down the broadcast equipment and kindly let us jump into their car. Safely back at our hotel, we looked like a bunch of circus clowns as we made our exit. Once again, the great people of curling to the rescue.

When we got back, we reunited with everyone at the hotel, although the celebration was somewhat muted. By this point everybody was exhausted, and the adrenaline rush from the finish was gone. Still, it was hard to sleep that night after what had been my greatest day in curling.

7

THE WORLD CATCHES UP

NOT LONG AFTER our win in St. John's, we were off to play the world championship being held in Paisley, Scotland, that year. After the heartbreak in juniors of winning a Canadian championship but never getting to represent Canada at the world championship, this was my first shot at a world title. It took us all a little time to come down from the high of winning the Scotties, but the thought of winning a global crown got us amped up pretty quickly.

So, too, did the arrival of our uniforms. Seeing the Team Canada jacket was a thrill. Just knowing we were representing our country and would play with the maple leaf on our backs was enough to send a chill down my spine. I will never forget the moment of seeing any of my Team Canada jackets for the first time.

For the 2005 world championships, the World Curling Federation decided to split the men's and women's events. For the previous 16 years, the two had been held at the same time in the same venue. Canada was willing to host a world championship every year, but the WCF needed to move the event around. Having two world championships (one for the men and one for the women) allowed Canada to play host every year. It made sense, especially when the events were held outside of Canada, where it was difficult to draw fans, especially for the women's championship.

When the decision was made, Colleen Jones quipped that women were going to have to do something big to attract any spectators. "I think the women are going to have to curl naked in order to get people out there," she said. "I'm not kidding," she went on. "You're going to have to hope for an Anna Kournikova to come along and really jazz it up."

I'm pretty sure Colleen was joking and we weren't about to play in the buff—even the baggy uniforms from the Scotties would be better than that—but she was correct about the dearth of spectators. Compared with the Canadian championship, the worlds that year was like playing at a local club. There were some fans, but nothing like we'd seen in St. John's—not even close. Most days, the fans consisted of our families and a handful of locals.

The poor ticket sales weren't the only issue for this event. Another was that the curling rink was part of a big sports complex, and it sat next to a swimming pool. Our change room was usually used by swimmers, and it didn't matter that the world curling championship was going on. While we were changing into our curling gear, women just a few feet away were putting on their bathing suits. And we couldn't put on our curling shoes because of the puddles all over the floor. That was certainly a first for me.

THE WORLD CATCHES UP

The pool created another problem because humidity seeped into the rink and made the ice frosty. At every draw, the frost would creep in from the sides of the sheet, making the playing surface increasingly narrow and heavy. In one game, the frost was so thick, we couldn't tell if our rock was in the eight-foot or the 12-foot circle because we couldn't see the colours of the rings. For those non-curlers out there, frosty ice is one of the toughest ice conditions curlers can run into. Imagine putting on your local golf course. Some parts of the greens have snow on them while others are rolling like the truest greens you've ever seen—but you can't tell which is which until you roll that putt. Challenging doesn't even begin to describe the problem.

And there was more. The organizing committee didn't use a water de-ionizer, a water purification process used in all big curling events and at most Canadian clubs. A de-ionizer makes the playing surface exponentially better, and the issues with our ice became so dire that the fourth draw was postponed so work could be done to try to improve the surface. I was shattered.

And even *that* wasn't the end of our problems. As the event began, most of the volunteers refused to help because they suddenly wanted to be paid. That meant a shortage of people at certain stations, one of which was running the time clocks. Umpires were then given the authority to pull a rock off the ice if they deemed there was a time violation, a highly unusual and arbitrary move by the World Curling Federation—and in my opinion, unacceptable. They wanted the curlers to keep up a pace of play, but you can't just create rules arbitrarily. But that seems to happen all the time in the amateur sports world— whatever suits that sports organization at the time. It seems like

ROCK STAR

this may be changing because athletes now have the ability to challenge a decision and ask why.

We didn't want to complain. This was our dream and what could be a once-in-a-lifetime opportunity. But it was difficult not to feel a bit sorry for ourselves. And we all knew these problems would never happen at the men's championship. If they did, the men would refuse to play. Truth be told, I was envious of how the men weren't scared to take a stand and stuck together to advocate for themselves. The women were not yet there and just accepted what was given to us.

Even with all this going on, we stayed positive and tried to focus on our game. As an athlete, I've learned there's only so much you can control. In curling, the conditions aren't one of those things. In most cases in Canada, we're spoiled by great ice and rocks and the best icemakers in the world, but sometimes you need to adapt. For me, letting the conditions get to you is detrimental. Instead of complaining about the ice, you have to adapt and accept. You need to have a love affair with the ice, even if you don't like it very much. It's hard enough to beat your opponent. Getting upset about something you can't control just makes life more difficult.

The event wasn't all terrible. There were lots of bright spots that week too. The people who were there, both volunteers and fans, were wonderful—and we made lots of great friends. Once again, we had great drivers. And instead of the usual rental vans at our Canadian venues, these folks used their own cars. One of our drivers had a Jaguar. Not great for carrying a curling team but certainly fun to drive around in. (We took turns as passengers.)

THE WORLD CATCHES UP

When we weren't playing, we took advantage of being in Scotland, visiting Edinburgh and stopping at the famous Carnoustie Golf Club. Those outings are great breaks in what is often a grinding week.

In spite of the conditions, our play in that event was fairly solid. We ended the week with an 8-3 record and finished in third place. For the first time at a women's world championship, the page playoff system was used. That meant we played the fourth-place team, Norway's Dordi Nordby, with the winner advancing to the semifinal. Sadly, our season came to an end when the Norwegians beat us rather handily.

It was a disappointing end to our year. After the high of winning the Scotties, not medalling at the world championship was heartbreaking. We now joined the ranks of Canadian teams that had lost at the worlds.

Canadian fans expect any Canadian curling team that plays in an international competition, be it the world championship or the Olympics, to win. For many, anything less than the top step on the podium is seen as a failure. Canada dominated the international scene from the 1960s through to about 2000 so handily that it seemed almost impossible for a Canadian team to lose. But the rest of the world was catching up and in some cases had already caught up. It's now as hard to win the world championship as the Canadian final. No matter where you're playing, there are no more easy games—especially when ice conditions don't allow the teams to really shine and show their abilities. The men would have walked off, as I said, but we just continued trying to be grateful for the opportunity.

ROCK STAR

WEARING THE MAPLE leaf was the proudest moment of my career, but it was stressful working my way up to that point. It seemed it was win or nothing else, and from the beginning I felt like I was fighting an uphill battle: Trying to be a leader for my team, even when conditions seemed impossible. Taking the high road and never complaining, even though an outcome wasn't remotely close to the dreams we had had for so long. The fairy tale was not a fairy tale at all, and there was not much we could do about it.

The media added to our stress. Its coverage was at times glowing and at other times harsh. When we lost our playoff game and were eliminated in Paisley, the media asked strong questions about why we lost. Some of the writers seemed only too happy to point out our mistakes. It was as if we could play well all week, then lose in the playoffs by a centimetre—and they would say we failed miserably.

This was my introduction to how hard the media could be, and the interaction left me reeling and running for cover. It wasn't the last acrimonious interaction I would have with writers and broadcasters.

The media members weren't the only ones to question us on losing a world championship. Regular folks back in Winnipeg and other places who would see these reports in newspapers and on local television would ask about our loss. How could a team from Canada lose to one from Norway? If we went to a charity outing that summer, we were asked not about winning the Scotties but why we lost at the world championship. In most cases, people were genuinely trying to be nice, but time after time, conversations began about the loss, not the win.

THE WORLD CATCHES UP

That took its toll on all of us. I felt like something of a failure and that I'd let my country down. Over the next few months, the response to our loss affected me emotionally. There were days when I felt very down.

As the off-season went on and we got closer to curling again, the questions and comments became fewer. I began to feel better and was able to put the negative comments behind me.

It helped that there were bright spots ahead. One was that our team would get to go back to the Scotties again, this time wearing Team Canada instead of Manitoba jackets. Knowing we would be back at the Canadian championship was a double-edged sword. On the one hand, we were able to prepare our curling calendar much more easily. We didn't need to worry about all the playdowns leading up to the Manitoba championship, and we knew exactly when we'd be leaving for the Scotties, which that year were in London, Ontario.

On the other hand, we wouldn't be arriving at the national final off a great run at the provincials, as would all the other teams. They'd be coming in hot; there was a danger we'd be coming in flat.

There was another major event on our schedule before that, however—one that kept us training hard in the off-season. The Olympic trials to determine the team for the 2006 Winter Games in Turin, Italy, were in early December.

After a 74-year absence, curling had returned to the Olympic lineup in 1998, and from that time on, rather than sending the reigning national champions, as many countries did, Curling Canada held a separate competition to determine the country's representatives. For most of the top players, this was a huge event. Not only did it mean a spot in the Olympics, but it was the hardest event to win. It wasn't just one team per province, like at the Scotties or the Brier. It was the best rinks in the country. For example, there could be three teams from Alberta. So this really was the deepest field in curling.

Teams built their schedules around making it to the trials. It wasn't just a one-year commitment—this was a minimum three-year build: working out, playing games, honing skills and doing everything to peak at the trials and become an Olympian.

Our team was no different in that respect. However, our lineup did have a change. In the off-season, Cathy Gauthier decided she couldn't balance all the parts of her life and have time for curling on the level we had committed to as a team. She was a mother and had a full-time job, so after reaching the pinnacle of Canadian curling, she decided to step away. She told us it was a hard decision, especially with the free pass to the Scotties, but she was confident in making the change.

I respected Cathy's decision and really felt she had her priorities in line. She knew it was time to step back and she didn't hesitate. Over the years, I've known many players who simply live, eat and breathe curling at the expense of the rest of their lives.

It didn't take long for word of an opening on our team to spread through the curling community, and we had lots of players reach out to apply for the lead position. One of those people was Georgina Wheatcroft, an exceptionally talented and experienced player. She'd won the Scotties twice and the world championship twice. She was also on the winning team at the previous Olympic trials in 2001. Her rink, skipped by

THE WORLD CATCHES UP

Kelley Law, competed at the Games in Salt Lake City and came home with a bronze medal.

Georgina wanted another shot at the Olympics, and she saw the opening on our team as the best chance to do that. She was so committed, she moved from her home in Vancouver to Winnipeg so she would qualify under the residency rules in place at that time. All the players on each team had to live in the same province.

We were ecstatic about getting this very talented and experienced player who had been down the road we wanted to travel. She brought with her an extraordinary work ethic. I thought we had worked hard over the previous few years, but now, with the chance to go to the Olympics on the line, that effort increased tremendously.

Georgina added a level of professionalism and even more accountability. No excuses. We were committed to the process and were prepared to be accountable to one another. It became our team creed. We would do everything possible to reach our goal of getting to the Olympics.

THINGS DIDN'T GET off to the best of starts. We'd planned a period of on-ice training in the summer. That meant we had to fly to Toronto to go to one of the very few clubs in the country that kept ice in during the hot months. The night before leaving, as I was packing, I began to feel ill. I knew I couldn't back out, not with all we'd put in place about being accountable.

I hoped the symptoms would disappear overnight, but when I woke up I still felt lousy. I called my mom, a nurse,

ROCK STAR

and explained my symptoms to her. She told me to head to the emergency at the local hospital. A friend of my mother's, a nurse named Nancy, would be there and Mom would alert her. When I arrived, Nancy checked me over and then did some bloodwork. I was waiting a long time for the results, and when I looked at my watch I realized I had to leave if I was going to make my flight. I told Nancy and headed out. I was still feeling awful, but I couldn't miss our first on-ice training session. I couldn't let my team down. That was the most important thing to me.

As I got into my car, I heard Nancy running after me, waving me down.

"You can't leave," she said, breathless but thankful she'd caught me. "Your white blood cell count is sky-high."

Sure enough, I went back in. After a few more tests, I was told I had appendicitis and needed immediate surgery. If Nancy hadn't caught me, I could have been on board that plane, my appendix might have ruptured (it had already started to leak, the surgeon later told me) and I could have died. Instead, I was in an ambulance heading to another hospital, where they performed the surgery. Even in that moment, I couldn't help feeling that I'd let my teammates down. The stitches from the surgery were barely in me and I was overcome with guilt, thinking I wasn't at the training session. As I've said, that's me, not wanting to let anyone down.

After the surgery, the doctor told me how very lucky it was that I didn't get on the plane. Yet there I was, worrying more about not being on the ice with the others. I always thought a good leader leads by example, and I still do. But there are

THE WORLD CATCHES UP

many examples to set. One is to ensure that you are happy and healthy enough to give everything to what you are doing. Putting yourself first will sometimes have the most positive impact on the people around you. It will also demonstrate that your teammates, family or colleagues should all do the same thing. I always thought putting yourself first was being selfish. But at times it is actually just being smart. This concept is something I continue to struggle with, and that struggle is a source of stress.

It took me a few weeks to recover from the surgery, but then I was back at it with full force. As the curling season started, our team, with Georgina on board, performed well. We felt good as we headed into December and the Olympic trials in Halifax.

This was a far different event than the Scotties or even the provincial playdowns we'd been in: only nine round robin games, and the field was deep. The prize was what every team had been striving for over the last three or four years. The playoffs were also different, with just three teams advancing instead of the usual four. The top team in the round robin went right to the final, with the next two playing in a semifinal.

The event started off well but then suddenly, during the night following our second game, I woke up in excruciating pain. I literally crawled out of my room and down the hall to knock on the door of our coach, Janet Arnott. Janet got me to the hospital, where it was determined that I had a kidney stone. That was very unusual for a woman of my age. Because drug testing was possible and pain medication was banned, I would not take anything. I was in agony. The stone was large, and I would need to undergo a procedure to remove it. It turned out to be blocking one kidney. I had a stent put in, and the removal would wait until the competition was over. I was so stubborn, I insisted on playing our morning game against Sherry Middaugh. I had vomit on my clothes, but I insisted.

Looking back, I can say that I let my team down in this moment. I was playing for them and for me, but my condition was a distraction and I should have stepped back. We won that game, but the distraction and emotional drain from what had taken place was too great. We went on a losing streak and found ourselves out of the playoffs.

We weren't as mentally tough as we needed to be and allowed this incident to affect our future performance. It was an important learning experience that we missed out on. We should have debriefed and, in the process, understood why we really performed poorly. Instead, we just said it was bad luck and moved on.

In February we put on our Team Canada jackets and played at the Scotties. We played well enough to make the final but lost to Kelly Scott. And that ended our reign as Team Canada.

It was also the end of that curling season, which was also the end of Georgina's time with us. She was firm on this being a one-year commitment, and she was headed back to BC. I learned a lot from her, including the deep attachment to the team that every player must have. She really made sure we were all on the same page, all working toward the same goals, all willing to put in the same effort. Encouraging us every step of the way, Georgina was never afraid of hard conversations, something I struggled with. Georgina would speak her mind,

THE WORLD CATCHES UP

and she never wanted to have any regrets. She was an athlete and treated curling as the Olympic sport it was.

And for the second year in a row, we were looking to fill a hole on our team. I have never been great at pushing forward a player at any time in my career. I prefer just to be a part of the group, hoping we can all get along and make a popular pick that suits the three of us. As always, that's me . . . just trying to keep everybody happy and not wanting to make waves.

However, this time, I changed. I decided I wanted to have my say, and I suggested we bring in Dana Allerton. Dana was one of my best friends at the time, and she was with me on my first Manitoba-winning team back in 2002. I thought she was more than capable of playing up to our level, and I wanted to do something good for her. I thought having her as lead would be a good fit.

Jill and Cathy agreed, and Dana came on board. I was ecstatic that my suggestion had gone through and overly pleased that Dana was on the team. But early on, it became apparent that this wasn't going to work.

Dana played well enough, but the team didn't mesh, and our early season events just didn't go well. There was tension, and it became difficult to communicate properly. So early in the season, we parted ways with Dana, and I was crushed at having let her down. I thought she would be a great lead, perfect for us. I would have a close friend on the team, and we'd continue to play at a high level. Instead, it was one of the worst moments of my life.

Dana was hurt when we told her it wasn't working. Her reaction was understandable, and so was the fact that she took it personally. For about 10 years after that, our friendship was affected, and there was a big hole in my life. That ate me up inside. I let her down, and I should never have jeopardized our friendship like that. I missed her terribly. As they say, you should never mix business with pleasure. I was trying to balance leadership for my curling team with a friendship, and I failed miserably. I felt totally responsible for everything, and the incident pushed me back into a shell. For some time, I didn't put forth any strong feelings on team-related issues. It was just easier to stay quiet and nod my head when the others made suggestions.

I'm grateful that Dana and I repaired our friendship after a long time-out, and we've put that dreadful episode in the past. She is one of the best people I know, which made getting inducted into the Manitoba Curling Hall of Fame with her, Jill, and Trisha such a special moment for us. It really meant the world to me. It was where it all began, and where my love of curling was allowed to flourish. These girls gave me so much. I know I let them down in some ways, but the moments and memories we created changed our lives.

Replacing a player in mid-season is never easy because almost every top curler is already committed to a team. We did have a good team in place and, with our record, the makings of a squad that could win Manitoba and return to the Scotties. Luckily, our coach was one of the best leads to ever play the game. Janet agreed to play the provincial playdowns with us because residency requirements had to be met. Once again, our team won the Manitoba playdowns, and we returned to the Scotties for a third consecutive year. We lost in the semifinal that year, but with everything going on, we were very happy with the result.

THE WORLD CATCHES UP

Janet was available for the Scotties, but we needed a player for the remainder of the season, including our upcoming trip to Bern, Switzerland. That's when Jill told us she had been in touch with Dawn Askin from Ottawa. Dawn was the second for Jenn Hanna when we won the Scotties in 2005. It was Dawn's rock that I used to ricochet off and take out their stone to win the title in dramatic fashion.

Dawn was planning on moving to Manitoba to be with her then-boyfriend, now-husband, Mike McEwen. She had asked Jill for advice on finding a curling team. It seemed like fate. We asked Dawn if she would consider playing a few events with us to close out the season, and she agreed. Our first trip was to Bern, and we had a blast. None of our luggage made it over, so we really got to know each other shopping for essentials, and we had never laughed so much. Moisturizer is my essential. However, my Swiss German is not very good, and I bought a face cream with sparkles in it. Let's just say I sparkled the entire time we were there.

With Dawn, it truly was love at first sight. To make life even better, Dawn literally did not miss a shot at lead, and we nicknamed her Super D. We even joked about buying her a cape. Dawn, who had never played lead before, embraced the position and in my opinion is the best lead to have ever played the game. She showed the world what owning a position should look like. She was a perfectionist and had a standard for herself that I had never seen before. She loved her role and wanted to be the best. Simply stated, she wanted to be part of a great team and fulfill her role to the best of her ability.

Dawn agreed to join our team full time for the following

season, with Janet returning as coach. And that's when the real magic began. Right from the start, Dawn fit into the lineup and played very well. She also fit into the team, becoming comfortable with all of us very quickly and buying into our team dynamic.

We had a great start to the 2007–08 season, and we rolled into the playdowns where we won the Manitoba title and headed off to Regina for the Scotties. Things didn't start so well for us this time as we split our first eight games, sitting at a record of 4-4. (To add a bit of excitement, our team van was side-swiped by a semi-trailer.) We knew one more loss would eliminate us, but we managed to find a finishing kick, winning the last three games and then two tiebreakers, a semifinal and the final.

We became known as the comeback kids who were never out of it. That's something Cathy Overton-Clapham brought to the team. She never believed we were going to lose, and she really fought until the end. The final was against Shannon Kleibrink of Alberta, a formidable opponent. We had a great tussle before stealing a point in the 10th end for a 6–4 victory.

Once again, we were on top of Canadian curling. And once again, we were off to the world championship. It was a home game this time, taking place in Vernon, BC. After the debacle of Paisley, it felt like a dream all over again getting to be Team Canada in Canada. We were beyond grateful for the opportunity.

Our hot hand continued and we rolled off wins in our first five games, eventually finishing at 9-2 and in a three-way tie for top spot. Our first playoff game was against Wang Bingyu of China. They'd defeated us in the round robin, and we met them again in the 1-versus-2 page playoff game. The result was the

THE WORLD CATCHES UP

same. They got off to a 4–0 start in the first three ends, and we were never able to catch up.

Thankfully, we weren't out. We dropped into the semifinal, where we beat Japan's Moe Meguro and earned one more shot at beating the Chinese team. The game against Japan was one I'll remember forever.

We gave up three points in the sixth end to really put ourselves in a bad spot. But then the comeback kids did their thing. Down three points in the ninth, we made a tricky run-back on my last shot for two points. The 10th end was looking bleak, but we made a perfect freeze on my first shot to set up a steal. It was one of the best shots I have ever made, though it's never talked about because it wasn't flashy. But it is one I will always remember. We went on to steal again in the extra end. It was a game where our will to win was too strong for us to lose. We came together and willed ourselves to victory. It felt powerful, and I have never been more proud of a team than I was in that game.

The fact that we were playing China in a world championship final was a story in itself. Curling was pretty much nonexistent in China before the sport became a member of the Olympic family in 1998. When that occurred, countries that had no experience in curling and, in some cases, no facilities began searching for athletes to take up the sport, with the goal of getting to the Olympics to represent their countries.

Wang began curling only in 2001 after being selected at an athlete identification camp in her home country. She and her teammates Liu Yin, Yue Qingshuang and Zhou Yan were

ROCK STAR

designated as the women's Chinese curling team and spent years learning the game and training to become Olympians. Most of this training took place in Canada, where the players would live for much of the winter. It was a remarkable story of dedication and perseverance. The fact that they were fully funded by the Chinese government was not lost on us or any other top Canadian curlers.

Playing the Chinese team in the final was a challenge. They'd defeated us twice already that week, and we were determined not to let it happen a third time. Most importantly, I wanted to win a world championship.

After dropping a point in the first end, we cracked a three-ender in the second, and after six ends, we were up 4–3. In the seventh end, they had one buried on the button and it looked like they might steal a point to tie the score. I had to play a very tricky shot, angling one of their stones onto one of our stones, driving that back to remove their stone in the four-foot. We executed it perfectly, allowing us to score two points. It was one of the most clutch shots I've thrown in my career, capped off by what my husband, Brent, now calls the "patented Jennifer Jones fist pump."

We finished things off by running them out of rocks in the last end to become world champions.

It was a complete performance. For the week, each of us was first in shooting percentage at our position, and we had a total team shooting percentage of 84 percent. I don't usually like mentioning percentages because I don't believe in them. What really matters are the shots you make when they are needed the most. Statistics are compiled by various people and can

THE WORLD CATCHES UP

be pretty arbitrary. Janet would keep our own statistics for training purposes, and they were never close to the statistics given by the statisticians at an event. However, it's rare that all four players are in top spot, and this statistic shows how strong our team was.

We celebrated after that win because there wasn't any need for planning meetings—unlike after winning the Scotties. But the win really hit home when we arrived at the airport in Winnipeg the next day. Hundreds of people were waiting to congratulate us as we entered the main terminal. Many were family and friends, but a great number were simply curling fans who wanted to celebrate with the team. It was a moment that was so Winnipeg, and something that made me so proud to be from Manitoba.

That moment was an incredible high. Unfortunately, what was coming in the days, months and years ahead turned that high into a low like I'd never experienced before.

8

ANYTHING BUT PERFECT

HEADING INTO THE 2008–09 season, Cathy, Jill, Dawn and I felt good about our play. We started out by winning the Wayden Transportation Ladies Classic, which was a Grand Slam event for the women that year. It always meant as much to me to win a Slam as it did to win the Scotties because the Grand Slam events had the best teams in the world competing, and you had to play your best to win. At the time they were as high profile as any event because the feeling of success was as great.

The Grand Slam of Curling is a series of the biggest curling events in the world, started in 2001 by a breakaway group of male curlers. This group included the likes of Kevin Martin, Kerry Burtnyk, Glenn Howard and many more. They had become frustrated with Curling Canada (then the Canadian Curling Association) and what they thought was an overbearing operation of the men's Canadian championship. Eighteen of the game's best curling teams boycotted the Brier and set up their own series of events called the Grand Slam of Curling. It took a few years, but eventually the women were added to the Slam events. We immediately put them on our tour schedule because they were worth more prize money and points in tour standings. At the time I remember feeling so grateful to the men who had started this series. They made sacrifices and took a stand for what they believed was right, and also for what they believed was best for the game, and we reaped the benefits.

One of the breakaway group's biggest beefs was that a team wasn't allowed to show its sponsors' crests during the Brier broadcast, traditionally the largest viewing audience of the year. So, for example, a top-ranked curler would get sponsorship from a car company. He'd wear its crest on his jacket all season long while playing in various big events, but when he got to the Brier, he wasn't allowed to have that crest on his uniform.

It meant curlers really couldn't get much for a sponsorship because outside of the Brier, the ability to show the sponsor's logo to a large audience was minimal. So instead of trying to battle with Curling Canada, the group created its own league, got Sportsnet to televise the games and allowed all crests to be worn and shown. In later years, it also meant they could play by their own rules, such as dropping the number of ends played from 10 to 8. The Grand Slams were started by the players and have always been loved by the players. They're where we try new things to make the game better. It's a place where you always feel valued and that your voice is heard. That holds true to this day. The Slams and Sportsnet's broadcasting of them changed the sport, and without them we wouldn't be where we are today. Their treatment of the players, our partners and our families has always been first class and made us feel like stars.

ANYTHING BUT PERFECT

The women got involved in 2006, and some of our biggest and most competitive tournaments were brought under the Grand Slam umbrella. This was huge for the women's game because it allowed us to play events with smaller but much deeper fields, and for bigger purses. We always wanted to hone our game against the best curlers in the world, and this allowed us to do that. The bigger prize purse took away some of the financial burden and made it possible to break even for the season.

However, even with the increased prize money in events, the cost of travel, coaching and entry fees was a huge financial burden for most teams. Capital One's Canadian operation came on as the title sponsor for the Grand Slam Series, and that's when things really started to change in women's curling. The women were initially included in the Players' Championship at the end of the year, which included the top 12 teams in the world. I was elated when we heard the news that the women were being included in the Players'. It meant arena ice conditions, playing against the best and being televised. A new place to showcase women's curling outside of the Scotties. Yes, we had deemed certain events to be Slams throughout the season, but those were played on curling club ice. All the top teams were there, but the event was not televised like the men's Slams. This was our chance to shine.

We went to the first Players' and I immediately thanked Capital One for including women. I met and had numerous conversations with their representative, Ian Cunningham, and we talked all things women's curling. Ian, who continues to be an incredible advocate, agreed that women's curling was ready to be showcased more and that the Grand Slams were the right platform. Capital One began talks with Sportsnet about including the women at all Grand Slam events. Curling had allies in Jennifer Kjell and Kristi Petrushchak, who were then responsible for the Grand Slam event operations for Sportsnet, and they ensured that when the women were added to the Slams, the prize purses would be equal for the men and the women. This was unheard of in most women's sports. It was the beginning of the incredible growth in women's curling.

We all owe a huge debt to the original men's teams who agreed to boycott the Brier and forgo their dreams for the greater good. They didn't boycott to help the women's teams prosper, but they knew what was needed for the sport to grow. We weren't a part of the boycott, but we used our voices and the platform that was created to ensure that the growth of curling also included the women. This was a time in curling that, in my opinion, was the most exciting. It was a pivotal time in the game's evolution. I really hope the players of today continue to talk about and thank those original "Slammers" for creating what have become the absolute best events in the world of curling.

To combat the boycott, Curling Canada created new events of its own with the Canada Cup and, eventually, the Continental Cup, which were prize purse events that TSN televised, allowing still more exposure for the game and for us as players. Curling Canada always claimed there was not enough money to pay prize purses at the national championships, but suddenly, after the boycott, it found the money to put on its own Canadian-only Slam-type event in the Canada Cup.

And then it came up with the Continental Cup, curling's

ANYTHING BUT PERFECT

version of the Ryder Cup in golf. This event pitted North America against the rest of the world. We loved the additional TV time and exposure, as the more we were on television, the more the sport could grow. In addition, curling associations in the rest of the world were putting more money and time into the game. With curling being an Olympic sport, and now with the Grand Slams being the best training ground in the world for top teams, regardless of nationality, these international associations knew they had no chance but to invest in the game and their athletes.

Some Canadians (including some Canadian coaches) started to express the idea that the Grand Slams hindered Canada's dominance in curling. I would argue that this was going to happen with or without the Grand Slams. The international teams were working hard and getting better. Plain and simple. The Grand Slams were for the players (all players) and to help grow the game so that perhaps curling could one day be professional. The Slams weren't created to fine-tune Canadian curlers' skills but, rather, to take curling to a new level of skill and visibility and increase its exposure around the world. I've always found that this Canadian-focused mindset totally misses the point on what needs to happen for curling to thrive around the world for many years to come. A leader must look to the future and not for immediate success.

During this time, we were definitely at the top of our game, and it was being noticed. In January, we were asked to do something a little different. TSN had been airing the Skins Game since 1986, and it had been exceptionally popular. Based on a golf game of the same name, it was a big-money made-for-TV event that awarded cash for each "skin" won. In the curling version, each end was a skin, and teams won it by taking two or more points when they had last rock or stealing a point or more when they didn't. If neither occurred, then the money was carried over to the following end. In 1996, TSN added a women's draw, with teams such as Heather Houston, Sandra Schmirler and Kelley Law taking part.

In late 2008, we received a call asking if we'd like to play. Of course we were thrilled to be able to compete on television for a chance at a big payout. But there was a catch: We wouldn't be playing women's teams. We'd be going up against three men's rinks. And it wasn't just any old men's teams; we'd be playing against the Kevin Martin, Glenn Howard and Randy Ferbey rinks, three of the best teams ever to play the game and, at that time, all at the peak of their skills. We agreed without hesitation, knowing our chances of success were slim. We didn't have the Skins experience these terrific teams had. Plus, men are stronger, and greater strength translates into more effective sweeping. But what a great experience for our team and women's curling. We didn't play well, but the guys were gracious and made us feel like stars. It was the biggest curling production we had ever been a part of—a single sheet at Casino Rama in Ontario—and it showed us where curling could go in the future.

Most fans believe that curling is one of the sports where men and women should be able to compete at the same level. Men do have a physical advantage in strength, making them superior sweepers. That strength also gives them the ability to throw the rock at a greater velocity, making certain shots easier. However, with the women's game becoming increasingly aggressive, we

ANYTHING BUT PERFECT

may see this change in the future. I am proud that Team Jones was at the forefront of pushing an aggressive style of play, and the Grand Slams were our training ground.

The 2009 Olympic trials had been at the centre of our bull's eye since the last one in 2005. Not only was making it to the Games the pinnacle of sport—not just our sport, of course—but the 2010 Games were going to be held in Vancouver. The chance to play in the Olympics in front of a home-country crowd was a once-in-a-lifetime opportunity.

It seemed like a perfect fit for us. We'd played well over the last few years, winning the Scotties in 2008 and '09. We were also world champions in 2008 and made it to the playoffs a year later.

We came into the 2009–10 campaign on a high, realizing we had this tremendous chance in front of us. We started the season well, winning a big international event in Oslo, Norway. It was far from an easy victory as we had to get by Anette Norberg of Sweden in the final, not to mention Switzerland's Mirjam Ott in the quarter-final and Eve Muirhead of Scotland in the semi (all were already, or would go on to become, world champions). Those were three of the best teams in the world, and for us to beat them all at one event showed how well we were playing at the start of the season.

That continued when we won the Autumn Gold Curling Classic in Calgary, one of the biggest events on the women's schedule. It was also part of the Grand Slam of Curling and had another very deep field.

But for some reason, as December and the trials neared, I felt we just weren't ready. That was almost preposterous

105

considering how well we'd played and that we were ranked No. 1 in the world. But there was a sense that our team really wasn't a team. We all played well and won a lot of games, but both on and off the ice, we weren't really meshing. In curling, winning a spiel or finding a hot streak doesn't mean a team is flowing perfectly. I've found that when you win, it's easy to put all the other issues on a shelf and deal with them later. *Problems? Don't worry about those. We just won another bonspiel.*

As we played events ahead of the trials, it seemed to me as if we'd lost our mojo. We were winning, but instead of the respect and sense of team, I felt some strain and friction. I wasn't pointing the finger at any one player or saying it was all aimed at me. Rather it was a team vibe I was sensing. As I always did in those situations, I didn't talk about it to Cathy, Jill or Dawn. I didn't want to rock the boat or upset anyone, especially with the trials so close.

Instead, I reached out to our support team of coaches and sports psychologists to see if they could help me unlock this mystery. Why, at this stage of our year, just when we were getting ready to play what could be the biggest event of our careers, was I thinking we just weren't ready? I was hoping they could help us do something different, help us change it up to revitalize our play. The support team felt that, because we were so close to the trials, we needed to work with what we had. So we went off to Edmonton, trying to figure it out on our own.

The trials that year were held at Rexall Place, the home of the NHL's Oilers. Edmonton is such a tremendous curling town that when the best teams came to play, they could easily fill the

ANYTHING BUT PERFECT

17,000-seat facility. It was a huge week for curling and for all the teams participating, both men and women.

Despite the team dynamic I'd wrestled with, once we got on the ice, we turned our attention to winning the trials and getting to wear the maple leaf in Vancouver. We came in with a lot of momentum, and most media reports seemed to have us as the favourites.

In our pre-event meetings and practices, we had focused on trying to be perfect. We wanted the perfect atmosphere, the perfect conditions and the perfect performance. Our goal was perfection.

But it didn't turn out that way. In fact, we were anything but perfect. This was the biggest event of our curling lives, and we played as poorly as we had ever played. We started slow and never recovered. Afterward, we tried to say the right things, but we were flat and nothing changed. To say we were disappointed is an understatement. I was devastated and felt like I'd let my team down. I knew something wasn't right, but instead of doing everything possible to fix the problem, I turned the other cheek and crossed my fingers. This is not a sign of good leadership or an athlete ready to go to the Olympics.

In hindsight, trying to be perfect was not what we should have been preaching. We'd learned that lesson at the world championship in Paisley, when conditions were out of our control. What we should have done at the trials, as we did in Scotland, was to accept everything as it was and play to the best of our abilities, which at that time was pretty good. Instead, we were trying to change things we couldn't alter—ice conditions,

ROCK STAR

rocks, strategy, shots from opposing teams, you name it. And when we started losing games, we began to get frustrated. It was a sad ending to what we had hoped would be a great week.

To me, it really came down to how we defined perfection. What we should have accepted is that perfection is only what we make it to be. Any environment can be perfect if we accept it as perfect. Instead of just playing the game as we knew we could, we were busy striving for something that was likely impossible to achieve.

Those were just my thoughts. I'm not sure what Cathy, Jill and Dawn were thinking, although we were all likely on the same wavelength. We never really sat down to debrief on the week. It was something we had done in the past and something we should have done in the aftermath of our collapse. I only know it felt as if our team's foundation was on shaky ground.

It would be four more years until we earned another shot at going to the Olympics.

FANS HAVE THE misconception that all the players on a curling team are great friends and spend curling and non-curling time together. Especially in women's curling. Although some of my closest friends have indeed been my teammates, at the highest levels, that isn't always the case. All of us have lives outside of the game and social circles that have nothing to do with curling. For me, those worlds are necessary for a balanced life. I curled better when it wasn't all-encompassing. I put a lot of time and effort into the sport—practice, training, games, travel and more. It's easy to get swallowed up in curling. Early on, I learned that

ANYTHING BUT PERFECT

stepping away regularly is necessary for some balance in life. That's where my lifelong friend Robyn, my work friends Nicole, Dayna and Marla, and my friends from the $20 Club, the group of women who met regularly for years, came in. To them I was Jen, and they didn't know much about curling. They didn't care if I won or lost; they cared if I was happy and smiling. Don't get me wrong—they supported my curling dreams and showed up to watch when they could, but the results weren't important to them. They supported me no matter what. Nicole made sure that flowers were waiting in my hotel room at all the big events I played in (and there were a lot back then). It was something Cathy and I looked forward to when we stepped into our room. I felt loved instantly.

The members of the team do need to get along and build a sense of trust in each other, but a curling team is sometimes more like a business. You come together for the success of the company, you have mutually agreed upon shared goals and you work to achieve them. There are lots of examples of successful men's and women's teams that stayed together simply because they were winning even if they weren't a well-functioning team.

There are also examples of successful curling teams that split up, and to the public, there doesn't seem to be any rhyme or reason. In those cases, it's usually less about curling skill and more about team composition.

Shuffling within a team is common in other sports, where a team is made up of people from different backgrounds and stages in their lives. A hockey team may have veterans who are married with children, and rookies who are just out of junior. Some players may be religious; others like the night life. A few players could be raucous, while others are quiet. The differences don't mean players dislike each other. What really matters is how they play as a team.

THERE WAS LIFE after the trials. Our team found its stride again and earned our third consecutive Scotties title, this one in front of a sold-out arena in Sault Ste. Marie, Ontario. It was a remarkable achievement to win three consecutive national championships. We were just the third team to accomplish that. It was also a boost to our curling egos in the aftermath of our poor week at the trials. I won't say the title healed all our wounds, but winning is a pretty good salve.

Between the Scotties and the world championship were the Vancouver Winter Olympics. Yahoo Sports asked me to jump from player to reporter and cover the women's Olympic competition. I leapt at the opportunity for a couple of reasons. First, I wanted to be at the Games and see and feel the atmosphere of an event I one day hoped to compete in. Second was that I wanted to understand what it would be like to report on curling rather than be the subject of the reports. It was an eye-opening experience on many levels (more on that later). I remember walking to the media bench and hearing Bob Weeks, a long-time curling reporter, say, "Welcome to the dark side." I laughed because it didn't feel so dark at the time.

I really enjoyed being on the media bench. Even so, the days were long and the food was terrible. Like, really bad. And there was no option to go anywhere else to eat. It was hard to get around at the Olympics, and the curling venue was not close to

ANYTHING BUT PERFECT

anything. With three draws a day, we were at the venue for 14 hours daily. We had chili almost every day until all the reporters got together to protest. The next day, the chili was replaced by shepherd's pie and we rejoiced. That is, until we realized they'd just thrown some potatoes on top of the chili. Food aside, it was an eye-opening experience, especially from a team dynamic perspective. I found it enlightening to watch teams function from a distance, and it was so easy to predict which teams would have success according to how they functioned as a unit.

After that, it was off to the world championship, which was taking place in Swift Current, Saskatchewan. We sailed through the round robin and lost just a single game, to veteran German curler Andrea Schöpp and her squad. Schöpp's team then came back to beat us in the 1-versus-2 game in the playoffs. We lost the semifinal to Eve Muirhead's Scottish team and had to settle for the bronze medal.

At that point, the team that had been fraying at the edges after the Olympic trials was starting to completely unravel. We had managed to avoid any discussions largely because of our play. Winning made it easy to kick the can down the road and deal with the problems the next week. Or the week after that. Or after the next event. Now that the season was over, we had to face our troubles head on.

My inclination, of course, was to get together, talk it out, solve the problems, make everyone happy, have a big group hug and start planning our next season. That's just my nature; if there's a problem, we can make it go away and everyone will be happy. But we were beyond that point, and deep down I knew it.

Janet, our coach, called a meeting, and we gathered in the

boardroom at my office. It went on for some time, and when it was over, Cathy was no longer a member of the team. It was a difficult end to our foursome, who had played so well for so long. We'd won big events all over the world, multiple Canadian championships and a world title. But when we left the boardroom, that team was no longer a team.

9

UP CLOSE AND TOO PERSONAL

WHEN THE NEWS of our team's lineup change filtered out, it became a big story in the curling world. That was understandable. We were the reigning Canadian champions, and to part with a member of our team at that time was shocking to most. That included the media, who were anxious for a comment. Jill, Dawn and I sent out a joint statement that we hoped would ease things. "Our goal is to represent Canada at the World Women's Curling Championship and the Olympics. To do that, we need to take steps now to ensure we will have a complete set of skills and strengths come 2014," it read in part.

The reports of the change were, for the most part, harsh. The media used words like *dumped*, *booted* and *chopped* to describe what happened. I was referred to as *cold* and *heartless*. In most of the stories, I was cast as the villain and sole perpetrator of the move, which wasn't true. I tried to understand that this was just a part of being successful, but it didn't make it any easier to digest.

That's a part of curling. When an athlete in another sport is

ROCK STAR

suddenly dropped from a team or traded, the general manager or coach gets the heat. That's his or her job. And while it can be shocking, that person isn't vilified as curlers are. When a pitcher is let go from a baseball team, the media don't go after the first baseman. In curling, it's almost always the skip who's called out, even if in many cases it's a team decision. I was prepared for the media's response and knew it was coming.

Up to that point, I had a great relationship with the press. And while several writers reached out and tried to present a balanced story, it seemed that many others were determined to cast the move as something that showed me to be a terrible person. At least, that's the way it felt. As well, I was still a private person at heart and didn't truly understand how the public or the media had a right to know personal and private conversations and thoughts. I've come to understand that we were in the public eye, and with that come many obligations and responsibilities, whether you want them or not.

There was another aspect to this situation. Some top men's teams had also made significant changes to their lineups, and the skips on those teams weren't labelled as nefarious. For some reason, I was "ruthless" while a player such as Kevin Martin was "progressive."

Martin's team broke up after the 2005 Olympic trials in which they finished with a lacklustre 4-5 record. It didn't seem as if he had to endure the glare of the spotlight or face the harsh questions as I did. Breaking up after just winning the Scotties was a hard reality for people to accept. But the Scotties was one event we played in, and we weren't looking to next year. We were focused on 2014 and the Olympics.

UP CLOSE AND TOO PERSONAL

It certainly felt as if my critics in the media were singling me out, or at least treating me differently, because I was a female. That wasn't the first and wouldn't be the last time that would happen in my curling career. What was even more frustrating was the different standard we as female athletes were held to. With friendship instead of competitiveness at the forefront. We were trying to put the best team forward to give ourselves the best chance of success, something both male and female competitors attempt to do. Our team didn't bring out the best in each other in the big moments, which is critical for success. A change had to be made. It wasn't personal; it just wasn't working. But for us, the negative comments were not focused on performance or the team but instead on how we hurt feelings. I can't remember a time when a change occurred on a men's team when feelings were even talked about publicly. It is a double standard that is impossible to live up to. However, things have evolved. In today's game not only are team changes commonplace, especially after an Olympic quadrennial, they even occur in the middle of a season without a second thought.

Over the years, I'd never felt comfortable being at the centre of the post-game scrum and looking out at a throng of reporters lobbing questions at me. Many times, they were demanding answers only moments after we'd just finished a game. But it was more than that. I honestly just didn't love the spotlight. I was always scared to say the wrong thing, or to have something taken out of context that might hurt a teammate or competitor. I have always had, and will continue to have, the utmost respect for my teammates and competitors. It was truly an honour to share the ice with them. But it seemed that all the media were trying to do was create a story—a rivalry or a conflict—because that is what sells. So for the most part, I was scared to say something wrong.

Between the post-game handshakes and my appearance in front of the microphone and lights, I really had no chance to gather my thoughts. For instance, if I'd lost a big game on the last shot, three minutes later I was trying to answer questions about what had happened. I hadn't even talked about it with my teammates, but there I was in front of microphones, notebooks and cameras, trying to explain what went wrong. I found that extremely hard to do and often tried to take some extra time to sort through my thoughts. But at events such as the Scotties or the world championship, the media officials tried to throw me into the scrum as soon as possible. I understood there were deadlines to meet and the story needed to go out, but that didn't make it any easier to deal with.

One of my best friends, Nicole, who is full of great advice that has helped me immensely, told me early on that if there is a story about you, good or bad, you must be doing something right. It means you are successful because people want to know more. Nicole liked to say that what the press writes is just words. But the relationships I have, and the people I surround myself with, are what's important. She always reminded me of my extraordinary friendships and of how much I was respected for the person I was.

EARLY IN MY curling career, most of the stories were almost like a fairy tale. We were the new kids on the block and could truly do no wrong. We were media darlings. I wouldn't say I was excited to talk to a reporter, but that I was honoured. I couldn't believe this shy little girl who loved to throw rocks on ice was being interviewed. It was something new and gave me a sign that I was on the right track. There was something exhilarating about it. I would read a story about myself the next day or see my face on the evening sports report on TV. That was big when we were just starting out. I remember recording the news broadcast on my VHS because I thought it would be the only one! I still have them today. Some of my favourites involved the great Joe Pascucci from Global Winnipeg.

As we continued to play better, it felt as if the writers were trying to probe a little deeper, to find out more about me and get past Jennifer Jones the curler. They were digging to put together a different angle or tell their readers something they didn't already know about my life. They questioned me about my family, my work, what I did in my social life, what I ate for breakfast and just about every nugget about my life, whether it had to do with curling or not. I understood that was their job, but I didn't like it. Why was anything about me other than curling relevant? Why was it fair that my life outside of curling was open for discussion?

That's when I first started to back off on the requests for interviews. I've always tried to be a private person. Once again, it's that introvert in me. I prefer to sit at home, alone with a book or a movie. Being on the sports pages or on SportsCentre when it was about curling was fine. I could talk about games and the goals for our team at the Canadian championship. But anything more than that made me feel vulnerable. I wanted my personal life to be personal, and sometimes I felt like I was losing control of that. While all of this was happening, I was going through some very difficult changes in my personal life, and that seemed to become fair game.

The better our team played, the harder it became. We'd do interviews on behalf of a sponsor or ahead of a national championship when we played as Team Canada. Organizers wanted us to try to raise attention for the event to drive ticket sales, so we'd hold a press conference, or a reporter would interview me over the phone.

In most cases, those interviews were fine, with predictable questions that weren't too hard to answer. But in interviews that dealt with our lineup change, I felt I'd been burned by a reporter who made some statements in the article that I thought were offside, bordering on the untrue. I was accused of being ruthless when we made the change and cast as cold-hearted in my approach to the game. That hurt me to my soul because curling was a love affair to me. I had a passion and true love for the game, and I didn't want to lose that joy.

In response, my guard went up. I became worried that every answer I'd give would somehow get twisted. I was scared to say the wrong thing and have the reporter paint me as someone I wasn't.

Gradually, I changed from a person who was excited about giving an interview into one who was terrified to step in front of a microphone or a tape recorder. I was suspicious of every reporter and every question asked. I was petrified to say something about a teammate or opponent for fear it would get twisted or taken out of context. Some reporters almost seemed to be laying

UP CLOSE AND TOO PERSONAL

a trap with the questions they asked and how they asked them, hoping I'd fall into it and give them more fuel for their stories.

It came to a point where I wanted to stop giving interviews. But that wasn't an option. It would be like throwing gas on the fire.

I stopped reading the sports section—in fact, I cancelled all newspaper subscriptions because I could no longer trust what I read. I also stopped watching the sports report on television. I thought that would help. But when a controversial story appeared, it was almost impossible to go anywhere without someone bringing it up or asking me about this piece or that headline. Whether it was at work or in the grocery store, it was inevitable. Everyone felt they knew me personally and had a right to ask any question. When that started happening with frequency, I knew something bad or embarrassing had been circulating.

Not every media person was harsh in their reporting. Many were fair in covering me and our team. There were indeed times we messed up. There were games where we missed key shots or made questionable calls. That was fair. I deserved to be called out for those. Even when we made a lineup change, there needed to be a response, which we provided.

But too often the articles were over the top. One said I had a reputation for "ruthlessly dumping teammates." Another said I was a "villain" because of the "cold, calculated manner in which we parted ways with Cathy." It started to affect me emotionally, and I withdrew. It was tough to be called terrible names and be described as an evil person. No matter where I went, I felt everyone was watching me and judging me. I was afraid to go out in public, and I relied on my close friends. They were exceptional for

119

me during this time. I would have been lost without the girls in my $20 Club, my friends at work (Nicole, Dayna and Marla), my friend since birth, Robyn, and of course my family. They would remind me that I wasn't that person described in the articles and would keep my spirits up, telling me the real Jennifer Jones was a kind person with a big heart whom they were grateful to call a friend.

We also had to do an Up Close and Personal at the Scotties, where we would gather after games in the larger bar area with fans and host Stu Brown—and the fans could ask any question they wanted. Again, they felt like anything was fair game. I was often asked why I didn't have any children. Followed up with "You're not getting any younger," and "Isn't family more important than curling?" Every single time, my heart would break into a million pieces. All I wanted was to have kids, but the time wasn't right, and these questions made me feel like a failure.

It took me a long time to come to terms with how the press too often portrayed me in a negative light. I felt incredible sadness that then turned to anger. I can't remember ever before feeling angry, but now I was angry for having my love of the game, and its purity, taken from me. As time passed, I became more secure in who I was. I ultimately became more comfortable in myself, especially after the birth of my daughters, Isabella and Skyla. I gradually began to realize that I liked who I was, and that's what mattered most. I am a good person, and if there are people who don't think of me in that way, then that's OK. I refuse to let someone else's opinion shape me, especially when I have never met the individual, and even more important, they have no idea who I truly am. They chose to believe the untruths

UP CLOSE AND TOO PERSONAL

they read. I can't make people see the person *I* think I am. I will always struggle with confidence and in feeling comfortable about myself. It's in my DNA. But our children have made me see the joy in every moment of life. I want them to see the world as a beautiful place that is not full of negativity or second-guessing.

As I said earlier, not every journalist was hard on me during these times. Many were fair in their reporting, even if I didn't always agree with it. That was all I really wanted: fairness. Many years later, one reporter apologized to me for some of the harsh things that had been written. I thought it took a lot of courage. Not many people have the courage to admit when they are wrong.

Gradually, I came out of my shell. I was more forthcoming with the media, and I said what I thought. I no longer worried about the ramifications of my words. I was being honest, and my teammates made me feel secure. They knew how I felt about them as people and teammates, no matter what was written. What more could I do? I finally realized I had the power to deliver the message I wanted. I was in control. I didn't need to respond to any question I felt was out of bounds. Or I could answer in a way that didn't expose anything I didn't want revealed.

It was uplifting, and I only wish I'd learned that all earlier. In some ways, I had allowed the media to steal my joy and love of curling. But not anymore.

10

DOWNHILL AND UPHILL

I ALWAYS KNEW I would go to the 2010 Winter Olympics in Vancouver. I just didn't expect to be sitting on the media bench, watching the teams I'd played against for the last few years battling it out on the stage where I wanted so badly to be. It was little consolation, but after flaming out at the Olympic trials, I accepted an offer from Yahoo Sports to provide reports on every round of the curling. I had always thought that after I was done curling, I would want to do some broadcasting, and this was a first step. It wasn't in the booth, but I was on the media bench and at my first Olympics live.

This opportunity gave me a brief foray into the life of a curling journalist and led to me spending time with many of those in the media who had covered my teams over the years. I wanted to be throwing rocks, not talking about them, but it was time to switch gears. It was difficult at times. There I was at the peak of my curling abilities, sitting behind the ice and kicking myself that I wasn't competing for an Olympic medal. It was a harsh reality to accept.

ROCK STAR

I remember walking into pre-event practice in awe of the facility and my heart sinking as I thought about what could have been. It was difficult, but then my attention turned to the pants worn by the great Thomas Ulsrud and his Norwegian team. They were flashy, with all sorts of wild and colourful patterns, like nothing that had ever been seen before in curling, where pretty much everyone wore black. Those pants made quite the statement and are still talked about today. It was interesting because after news broke about "the Pants," I was asked by my boss at Yahoo why I hadn't written a story about them. It was the first time I had been on the other side as a journalist—and I didn't realize fashion was an important subject for a sports reporter. I felt like I had failed, but I also didn't understand why it was a story. Then I started wondering why nothing had ever been written about the see-through pants female curlers had been forced to wear, with the hot pink panties showing through. *That* was a statement!

There were, however, some benefits to the job. I got a chance to watch great teams perform from a totally new perspective. And what became clear very early on were the differences between those who had it and those who didn't. I could tell from pre-event practice which teams were going to compete for the medals and which were going to finish down in the standings.

The "it" wasn't so much about the ability to throw a stone or call a game—it had to do with how players carried themselves on the ice, how they communicated with each other and how they functioned, both individually and together. The players knew their roles, knew how the team worked as a unit and understood what they had to do to win. They were one another's biggest

DOWNHILL AND UPHILL

cheerleaders. Even though it was the Olympics, they didn't look nervous at all; they looked ready to perform. They were enjoying the moment—and each other—and we could all see it. These were the things that set them apart.

My team at that time was good at all those intangibles, but deep down I knew we had to be better if we wanted to ensure we were at the next Olympics. We could go head-to-head with any rink in the world (we were ranked No. 1 in the world at the time) and probably had beaten the contenders more often than not, but we needed some of those things I was seeing on the ice in Vancouver. We needed to find a way to bring out the best in each other when it mattered most, when the pressure was on. We needed that sense of complete support, togetherness and joy.

Curling had advanced so much since it returned to the Olympics in 1998 that it wasn't enough to be good at throwing a rock. Participating countries were pouring lots of resources into improving their curling teams, hoping the investment would produce a medal. Advances in training, nutrition, equipment, sweeping and just about everything else moved ahead quickly, with everyone looking for an advantage. That's what the Olympics brought to curling, and no one wanted to be left behind. There are many Canadian curlers who believe the Olympics changed the Canadian curling culture. And that wasn't a compliment. The Olympics definitely changed the time and commitment required to compete at the highest level, but they also helped curling be seen as the sport it was. Curling gained respect, and the athletes had to work harder. I am not sure this is a bad thing. Curling made it to the Olympic stage, but we must work to ensure that the joy of curling at the grassroots level never dies.

ROCK STAR

There were also countries where curling had never been a big sport (if one at all) where it grew at the elite levels. Many of these teams were state funded and curled full time. Most of that time was spent in Canada, where the facilities were plentiful. The players would be on the ice or in the gym six to eight hours a day. That's the sort of commitment that led to what I saw on the ice in Vancouver, and it didn't worry me. In fact, it made me even more energized about the next four years and the prospects of being in Sochi wearing the maple leaf. I was ready to put my full focus and commitment on reaching that goal.

The first step toward achieving that objective was bringing Kaitlyn Lawes into the fold when the season ended. After the difficult parting with Cathy, we knew we needed to focus on our team dynamics—how we functioned as a unit. With a new player, we had added a new part to our machine, and we wanted to make sure it was going to run smoothly. That meant compatibility both on and off the ice.

I don't remember the first time I met Kaitlyn, but I would run into her father, Keith, when I'd pop into the Valour Road and Fort Rouge curling clubs in Winnipeg. He would always tell me about Kaitlyn's latest adventure and how she'd done. He was a proud father and was always praising his daughter's achievements and boasting of her talents, as you'd expect any parent to do. He reminded me of my dad, which is the biggest compliment. He would shine with pride when he spoke of Kaitlyn.

After finishing her junior career, Kaitlyn played third for Cathy King in Edmonton for one season. We'd run into Kaitlyn and Cathy at various women's events and in the Grand Slams, where we'd play against them occasionally. Kaitlyn was a very

126

DOWNHILL AND UPHILL

impressive player for someone so young, and she caught our attention. She was highly skilled, seemed fearless on the ice and appeared to have a personality that was just what we were looking for.

I wasn't the only one who noticed Kaitlyn's talents. Dawn and Jill were equally captivated by her play. But the three of us wanted to take our time and discuss what we wanted in a new player and make sure we were all on board. This was a big commitment, and we wanted to get the best possible person, not just as a curler but also as a teammate. With that in mind, we had a joint brainstorming session, went over a number of possibilities and drew up lists. And at the top of all our lists was Kaitlyn Lawes.

Of course, just because we were sold on her didn't mean she would be interested in playing with us. I gave her a call and asked if I could meet her when I was on a business trip to Edmonton, where she was living at the time. I felt this conversation was important enough to take place in person. I wanted to look her in the eyes and see her reaction to the offer to join the team. I needed to know that she was going to fit in with the rest of us. I wanted to see if she had the sparkle in her eye, which my dear friend and long-time teammate Jennifer Clark-Rouire said was essential.

We agreed to meet at a hotel restaurant. Heading to the rendezvous, I'm pretty sure I was as nervous as she was. As soon as we started talking, I could tell that she had everything I wanted in terms of personality. It didn't take Kaitlyn long to say yes. She was so excited to play, to get better, and was driven and focused to reach the goal of the Olympics. Being a bit younger than the rest of us, she could bring some youthful energy to our

ROCK STAR

team. A different perspective, I always say, is the key to success. She hadn't gone through a lot of what we had, so there was also a sense that everything was new to her and she was eager to learn. She had that sparkle we were looking for, and she sounded like she'd be an incredible teammate.

Kaitlyn's integration into the team began right away. At the start of every season, our team liked to play in a bonspiel in Europe. There were two reasons for that. The first was that it allowed us to compete away from the big stage and media scrutiny in Canada, and the second was that it provided a great way to enhance the team chemistry.

As part of our European trip, we always added a bit of a holiday where the four of us would play tourists for a few days, visiting places such as Paris and London. As much as we travel during a season, it's rare for us to go sightseeing in the destinations where we play, so our trip offered a great opportunity. Jill and I have always had the travel bug, and because of curling, we have seen most of Europe together. I am so grateful for that time with Jill and the memories we made. Jill and I loved doing the same things and had so many laughs. From Paris to Bruges, I loved every moment. Those trips are among my fondest memories.

With team bonding and team chemistry such a big focus for this new team, we all decided to travel together to our first spiel in Europe, which happened to be in Norway. We wanted to start off by creating a great team energy—and what better way to get to know each other than to travel together. We decided to start off with a pre-Norway stop in Turkey.

At dinner on our first night, I expressed to the other three

DOWNHILL AND UPHILL

that we should be prepared for the fact we might not be very good in our first year. Not, of course, because Kaitlyn wasn't up to the task, but because as a new team we were going to need some time. I also said I wasn't worried. We had a four-year plan in place, and year one wasn't necessarily about winning every game. It was about creating our team identity and personality. We needed to find our secret sauce, what made our team special, and create a sense of "teamness"—a word we created for this purpose—that would stand the test of time.

Every curling team has a personality. To outsiders, it might seem as if all four players are like a big family, but that isn't always the case. Some are like businesses, where you play your games but don't necessarily hang out together afterward. Others can be made up of players who get along off the ice but not necessarily on the ice, disagreeing over shot calls or strategy.

It can also be difficult when you aren't winning. That's often the time when the true makeup of the team is revealed. Tensions rise, players begin to point fingers, games finish and everyone goes their separate ways.

I've been on teams like that, and while you can win, it's no fun. During the season, players spend an inordinate amount of time together. You are with your teammates more than your family, travelling, curling and practising. I think it's hard for a team that doesn't have a great chemistry—or "teamness"—to be successful over any length of time. That's why I was so excited when we sat down for our first dinner that year in Turkey. I knew immediately that we had the four perfect people.

Although Kaitlyn hadn't even thrown a rock with us yet, I could tell we were perfect for each other. It was as if we'd played

ROCK STAR

together for 20 years. None of us could believe how easy it felt. We laughed and were vulnerable. We were all different people, but we respected our differences and knew they were going to prove a strength. We could use each other's perspectives to never miss a beat and to ensure we always thought outside of the box. Most importantly, we knew instantly that we had each other's backs.

Very quickly, we all found it easy to be authentic with each other. In my mind, this is key. I've played on teams where that never happened, where we couldn't all be honest and completely open with one another. When it became clear we shared that trait of authenticity, it became very powerful.

It wasn't just about Kaitlyn either. I felt that Dawn and Jill were as relaxed and positive as I'd ever seen them. They had that sparkle in their eyes. The joy and childhood enthusiasm they had for curling was back. Something just clicked immediately, and it felt like magic.

When we decided to add Kaitlyn, I hoped that by the end of the first year we would have created great team chemistry. That was my only goal for the year. I wasn't worried about results, but we needed our secret sauce and to create a strong sense of team. Miraculously, we achieved that goal by the end of September. All it took was the trip to Turkey.

On the ice, our first year together was very good. We led the 2011 World Curling Tour Order of Merit and went back to the Scotties as Team Canada. We made it to the final before losing to Saskatchewan's Amber Holland. The game came down to the last shot, which I thought I had made. That is a loss that still hurts my heart. We were so close, but it just wasn't meant to be.

DOWNHILL AND UPHILL

The fans at the Scotties were challenging—they let us know they were still unhappy about our parting ways with Cathy. But their response actually made us stronger. We stuck together and lifted each other up in a way I didn't think possible. Losing is hard, but I think being so close, dealing with fan adversity and handling a difficult loss made us stronger as a team and, in the long term, helped us to be successful. While it was hard to get so close and not win, our year went pretty much according to plan.

In 2012, we won the Manitoba playdowns and made it back to the Scotties, this time losing in the semifinal to Heather Nedohin and her Alberta foursome. Again, we were disappointed not to go further, but all in all, it was another successful season. We topped the Order of Merit once more.

Two years into our four-year plan, I was thrilled by what we'd achieved and how our team was performing. The next season, 2012–13, would be the most important for our team. We would be working to secure our spot in the Canadian Olympic trials, which would take place in December 2013. That was where Canada's Olympic representatives would be decided. It was also when we needed to hit our peak performance, to be at our absolute best.

But everything we'd worked for and all our successes to that point almost came to a crashing halt.

I was in a relationship with Brent by that time. He curled with Glenn Howard out of Ontario. Brent is the best thing to ever happen to me. However, with residency rules the way they were, we were essentially forced to live apart. He lived in Ontario with his son, Wil, whom I adored, and I lived in Manitoba. We were long distance and saw each other when we could, but it was difficult, and I wished the residency rules would have been different. Other sports weren't governed by residency requirements—it was just curling. If you mentioned anything about this to curling fans, they'd tell you to find a different team. But both of us were on teams ranked very high in the world, and we both made four-year commitments and couldn't walk away from our squads. Brent had a son in Ontario, and I couldn't just bolt from my team in Manitoba. This meant we had to be apart.

After our Scotties loss, Brent's team won the Brier. It was an absolute thrill to be there and watch him celebrate that amazing achievement. The victory meant they would represent Canada at the world championship in Basel, Switzerland. Because we'd both been through the intensity of the Canadian championships, Brent and I flew over a bit early to have a short vacation together, spending time in Grindelwald and Zermatt.

On our first morning there, we decided to go skiing. Skiing is probably not something a curler who is gearing up for the final stage of an Olympic run should have been doing. In fact, I didn't tell anyone I was skiing—I'm sure they would have said I was nuts for taking that risk. One slip and everything would be over. But it was a much-needed couple of days off, and we weren't on the double black diamond run or anything too demanding. It was essentially a bunny hill that anyone who has skied could handle.

Anyone but me, that is.

As I pushed off from the top of the hill, I hit a bump, my leg twisted and I felt a jarring in my knee. I knew almost immediately that I'd done something bad to it. Really bad. Still, I told myself it was nothing and went down the hill four or five more

DOWNHILL AND UPHILL

times. Despite the pain, I tried not to think about it. Some Advil and a little rehab, and I'd be fine.

It was also the first day of our trip, and I didn't want to ruin anything. I put one of those HotShots pocket warmers on my knee, trying to convince myself that would help. We kept doing what we'd planned to do, and I tried to hide the severity of the pain. In fact, I continued to ski the next three days. But deep down, I was worried.

By the time we got to Basel, my knee was very swollen and I was having a hard time walking. I was also a mess emotionally. I kept telling Brent that all I could think about was how I'd let my team down and how stupid I was to go skiing. We'd made all these sacrifices as a team, and now I'd ruined it all. I was even wondering if I'd ever curl again. I thought my career was over.

When we got to the world championship, I went to see the event's medical staff, headed by Dr. Weisskopf, who happened to be an orthopaedic surgeon. He took one look at my knee and said I needed an MRI.

My experience told me I'd probably be waiting weeks or months before I'd be able to get in and have that done, but not with Dr. W. We got into his car immediately and drove to a facility where I had an MRI with contrast. (A dye is injected into your arm, then it travels through your body to enhance the image. It allows for a much better diagnosis. That didn't mean anything to me at the time but would become important a few weeks later.) The imaging showed I'd torn my ACL, MCL and meniscus. Essentially, my knee was ruined. I would need surgery and probably a long rehab.

ROCK STAR

I stayed on in Switzerland and did some television commentary for the World Curling Federation, hobbling from place to place and trying to keep anyone from finding out about my knee. I hadn't told my teammates or family—the only people who knew were Brent and Dr. Weisskopf.

Before I left Switzerland, I did two things. The first was to reach out to Gerry Peckham, the head of high performance with Curling Canada. Gerry had been one of the most influential people in our team's career, helping us with all the resources the association offered.

Gerry's one of the few people I've trusted implicitly throughout my career, and trust doesn't come easily to me. But Gerry's always proven I could trust him. He keeps things in confidence. And he's always there to support you and give you a hug when you're down. Once I trust you, you're in for life. It's just how I work. I knew I could discuss my situation with Gerry.

He put me in touch with Dr. Robert McCormack, an orthopaedic surgeon in Vancouver who was Curling Canada's chief medical officer. I went to see Dr. Bob, as we called him, as soon as I returned from Switzerland. It didn't take him long to agree with the first diagnosis. My knee was a disaster, and I'd need surgery.

AS IT TURNED out, my knee wasn't the only change in my physical condition. I began to have some indications I might be pregnant. I bought a pregnancy test and, yes, I was having a baby. That, of course, was an incredible change in the big picture. I loved being

DOWNHILL AND UPHILL

a stepmom to Wil, and it made both Brent and me realize how much we wanted a baby. But to date, it hadn't happened.

Curiously, just a few weeks earlier, a rumour started circulating at the Brier that I was pregnant. I had to answer so many times that I wasn't, and to listen to so many fans tell me I wasn't getting any younger. A fact I was very aware of. It just made me sad because I really wanted to conceive. (One of the most difficult things about being in the public eye is having to face personal challenges publicly.) So when it did happen, people thought I had not been truthful and let me know they were disappointed I had lied. But I can confirm Isabella was conceived in Switzerland. And for that reason alone, Switzerland will always be one of my favourite places in the world.

After finding out that my dream of having a baby was finally happening, reality started sinking in. When we worked back the dates, it became clear that I was likely a few days pregnant when I had the MRI in Switzerland. I was worried that the dye injection might have harmed my baby. I instantly felt the mom worry that stays with you for a lifetime. A new, very scary, but also incredible feeling.

When I told Dr. McCormack the news of my pregnancy, he suggested I wait until after I had the baby, which was due in December, and then fix my knee in January or February. (There were risks—for both the baby and me—if surgery took place while I was pregnant.) The recovery would take a full year, he said.

With those words, my heart sank. That would mean I wouldn't be ready for the Olympic trials, which were scheduled

ROCK STAR

for the middle of December. I couldn't just show up at the trials after a year off and expect to compete, but that's what it would mean.

I have never taken no for an answer, and I always believe there is a solution to any problem. I asked Dr. Bob if there was any other option, something that would let me have my baby and my knee surgery in time to let me curl again. I wanted it all, though it began to seem like that wasn't going to be possible.

There was one way, he explained. I could have the surgery at the start of my second trimester, but there would be a hitch—I wouldn't be able to have a general anaesthetic. Instead, I would be frozen from the waist down and remain awake throughout the entire process. As well, I wouldn't be allowed any pain medication after the surgery. The most I could have would be a regular Tylenol. Also, Dr. Bob worked out of British Columbia, so I would have to fly there and stay for two weeks because the risk of blood clotting was much higher for pregnant women.

My first thought on hearing these conditions wasn't that they were scary or that I'd have a lot of pain. It was that there was a way to have the best of all worlds. In my head, I could hear that line by Jim Carrey from *Dumb and Dumber*: "So you're telling me there's a chance."

I could have my baby, fix my knee and get back on the ice in time to be ready for a shot at the Olympics. It meant I wouldn't let my teammates down. From a curling standpoint, that was the biggest part of this news. If there was no risk to the baby, it was an easy decision to make.

With that settled, I had to attend to the second task, and that was telling my teammates what I'd done. I'd kept them in

DOWNHILL AND UPHILL

the dark long enough. And so I arranged a meeting at Kaitlyn's house. We sat in her sunroom, and I spilled my guts. I told them everything—from how I'd wrecked my knee to how I was now pregnant. All they did was smile and give me a big hug of congratulations. They knew how much I wanted a family. They were supportive and never looked worried. (Even though, to be honest, I was a little nervous inside.) I couldn't have asked for a better reaction from my team, and I'll always be grateful I had them by my side.

They were surprised by the lengths I was going to go to so I could rejoin them, but I could tell they didn't doubt me. And that was exceptionally encouraging. I thought they'd be behind me, but it was amazing to hear them pledge their support and know they'd be willing to adjust our long-term plan to accommodate me. A load had been lifted off my shoulders.

This was another example of what made our team so strong. We had each other's backs. I was asking a lot of them, to wait for me and hope that when I returned, I could still play as I had in the past. They were behind me 100 percent.

I had to make one more call.

Right before I left for Switzerland, our team had agreed with World Financial Group that they would be a partner and support our Olympic dreams. Despite what many believe, competitive curling is expensive, and without partners we wouldn't have sufficient funds to travel to events. This partnership would allow us to compete at every event we wanted to. It was a handshake deal with the group's president, Rick Williams, and nothing had been inked yet. I had to call Rick and let him know what had happened and that I was going to miss at least half of the curling season. I was scared he was going to back out, and to be honest I wouldn't have blamed him. But the first thing Rick said to me was "No problem. What can we do to help? Jennifer, our motto is that no family is left behind, and we won't leave you behind." I was in awe and will be grateful to the end of time. If Rick Williams messages me and needs something, my answer will always be yes.

THE SURGERY WAS scheduled for June in Vancouver. By that time my pregnancy was giving me a heavy dose of morning sickness, which only added to the list of things I had to deal with. Dr. Bob performed the operation, and I remember every single part of it, from the first incision to the last stitch to close up my rebuilt knee. As I lay on the table watching the doctor and nurses huddled around my leg, hearing the machines and tools whirring, and at times seeing smoke rising, I asked myself if I had thought this all the way through. By that point, of course, it was a little late to change anything. I was pot committed, as they say.

Dr. Bob pronounced my surgery a success, and rehab started almost right away. I was told the faster I started rehabilitation toward getting full extension and flexion in my knee, the higher the chance of regaining full mobility, which I needed. Just 18 hours after the pieces of my knee were put back together, I started the exercises that would give my leg full function.

The other thing that started quickly was the pain. When the spinal anaesthesia wore off, a massive wave of pain kicked in.

DOWNHILL AND UPHILL

I wasn't expecting it to be that strong, and it was hard to manage. But I remembered what my parents had always said to me, that there is nothing we can't do if we put our minds to it. That was my mantra from the time I was young, and now I really had to focus on it.

I've never been afraid of pain, but giving up and being satisfied with mediocrity was something I couldn't accept. I had come this far and given my best. Battling through the pain was just another hurdle on the way to the Olympics. I couldn't let my team down, and I wasn't going to let myself down either.

More importantly, I was also about to become a mother, and setting an example for our baby was something I thought about a lot. Pain? It would just make everything else so much sweeter when I got through this. I was quite the bundle of fun at this point—swollen knee, in agony, pregnant and puking and undergoing physio that felt like it was killing me. Anyone who ever says curlers are soft should have been there the day after surgery.

I spent two weeks in Vancouver recovering, the first week with my mom, Carol, at my side helping, and the next with Brent. In addition to a hundred other daily tasks, they had one more unpleasant job. Because I was pregnant, there was the risk of blood clotting after the surgery. My caregivers had to give me daily shots of heparin, an anticoagulant.

I'm not sure who dreaded it more—Brent and my mom or me. The needles burned when they entered my stomach, and eventually that area just became one big, dark bruise. I don't know what I would have done without those two looking

ROCK STAR

after me. They did everything they could to ease my situation and made it possible to finally travel home, where the assistance continued.

I applied ice to my knee to help reduce the swelling, and at one point Brent set up an ice machine on the dresser beside my bed. But one morning I rolled over in bed and somehow caused the machine to come crashing down on my head, adding to my collection of aches and pains. Brent was also in charge of the bucket brigade. My morning sickness hadn't let up, and with my leg still stiff and sore, there was no way I could make it to the bathroom in time when I had to throw up. So he'd be at the ready with a bucket to catch it all and then dispose of it.

While all this was happening, I was committed to my daily rehab sessions. I often had to push myself to go—it would have been easier just to stay in bed. But I knew that the more diligent I was with this work, the better chance I had of getting back on the ice. It was a slow, gradual progression, but I could see and feel the improvements.

Up to this point, only a handful of people knew what was happening. I told only those who absolutely had to know. I tried to keep my situation as quiet as possible for a variety of reasons. First, I didn't want to let our opponents think I was vulnerable and give them a perceived mental edge over us. If they thought my knee wasn't great or that I wasn't at my best, that could help them. As I look back, though, I think I was scared that if more people knew, it made my difficulties more real—and more possible that my situation would be career ending.

Second was that I felt the media had excoriated our team after we'd parted with Cathy. Everything we did, every move we

DOWNHILL AND UPHILL

made, seemed to be scrutinized heavily by the press—and usually the stories showed us in a negative light. If the media found out I'd had surgery while pregnant, I'm sure they would have blown the story up and people would have judged me. Having a baby was my lifelong dream. I didn't want media comments or public perception to ruin my excitement.

Despite my being reticent around the press, the situation almost leaked out. A few weeks after returning to our home in Ontario, I had to fly to Winnipeg on business. I was still on crutches and a little wary of anyone seeing me. As I exited the airplane, I got into a wheelchair being pushed by an Air Canada concierge, who was incredibly kind—and my friend. We were moving through the airport when I saw the Winnipeg Blue Bombers all getting off a plane at a gate ahead of us. Some of the sportswriters who had been covering the game must have been on the same flight, because right ahead of me was Paul Wiecek, a writer for the *Free Press* who also covered curling. If he saw me in a wheelchair, my cover would be blown. I told the concierge to move me as fast as he could away from there, and he raced me off into a corner where I wouldn't be seen. Thankfully, the sprint got me out of Wiecek's line of vision, and I was safe from being a story in the next edition. We laughed, and my friend said presciently, "Maybe this story will make your book when you write it one day."

For the next few months, I did very little except try to recover. I went to rehab every day and did anything I could to allow my leg to heal. But I also stuck diligently to the program my physiotherapist set out for me. He knew I was anxious to progress as fast as I could, but he warned me that this was going

ROCK STAR

to take some time, and the best thing I could do was follow his program—no more, no less. Anything else could result in a setback.

My physiotherapist said it would likely take six months until I'd be able to curl again. But that wasn't going to cut it as far as I was concerned. I needed to be ready well before then. I buckled down and placed my entire focus on strengthening my knee. My days were basically rehab and throw up, rehab and throw up.

There were also a few complications not directly connected to my knee but more logistical in nature. It was my right knee that was injured, so that meant I couldn't drive. I had to rely on a team of chauffeurs made up of Brent, my mother and my in-laws. They took me to every appointment, whether it had to do with my knee or the baby. I was also commuting regularly, coming to Ontario to see Brent and then going back to Winnipeg to work and see my obstetrician.

The hard work paid off, however, and in August, just two months after my surgery, I stepped back onto the ice for the first time. It may sound strange, but when I took that first slide I had tears in my eyes. After all I'd been through, it was incredibly emotional to know I was back on the ice. During the ups and downs after the surgery, I honestly wondered if my career was over. But there I was, feeling the ice, smelling the rink and feeling the breeze as I glided to the hog line. To me, I was home. At that moment, I knew I was going to be OK, and going to the Olympics was still a definite possibility.

I think that staying positive throughout this entire episode helped me get back to where I belonged. I have always believed

DOWNHILL AND UPHILL

that we control our attitude, and that our attitude controls our destiny. My return to the ice seemed to prove that belief. Of course, it helped to have so many other people on my side—family and friends—helping and encouraging me.

And none of this would have happened if not for Dr. McCormack believing in me and giving me the option to have the surgery while pregnant. I put my trust in him and never doubted he would guide me on a safe path. While I still had a long way to go before I would be on the ice in a competitive event, my Olympic dream was still alive. Even more importantly, I was about to become a mother.

PRIOR TO MY surgery, I had an interaction that left me stunned. I was put in touch with a private group that could potentially help me out with the costs associated with rehabilitating my knee. (I won't reveal the group's name or any of the individuals involved.) It felt like a dream come true.

I had a call with one of the people involved, and we had a long chat. I told him of my injured knee, and he said he believed they could help. He added that the group would also help the entire team and give us access to all their specialists. It almost seemed too good to be true. I felt a weight lifted from my shoulders. I could potentially be ready to make a run at the Olympics. A short time earlier, I thought I'd let my team down. Now I was welcoming this knight in shining armour to save us all.

Not long after that discussion, I had an in-person meeting

143

ROCK STAR

with the same man. After a few pleasantries, I updated him about my knee and then revealed that I was pregnant. His first question to me was shocking:

"Do you plan on keeping the baby?" he asked.

It was strange to me because the question came without any hesitation. It was as if he had asked it before or that it was commonplace. To me, it was a very personal question and not one you would ask someone so directly. I told him I most definitely did, and how I had wanted a baby and was overjoyed by my pregnancy. I also told him more about the surgery and how it would proceed. He responded by saying that another athlete they had worked with chose a different path and had had an abortion. She felt her sport was more important at this point in her life, he added.

My jaw dropped, and I could tell that was the end of our conversation. I respect the right of every woman to make decisions over her body, but it was clear to me that in this situation, my own choice would not be respected. There I was, being judged for wanting to keep my baby. Without saying the words, I was being told it had to be one or the other. What it should have been was a celebration of someone working to become an Olympic athlete *and* a mother at the same time. To me, that would be an achievement worthy of supporting. It was certainly something Brent was never asked about when I was pregnant with Isabella. He did not have to choose. It wasn't that long ago that I was unfairly criticized in the media for being "ruthless," and now I was being criticized for wanting to have a baby. It made me realize that in the world of sport at the time, it was often a no-win situation for women, full of double standards.

DOWNHILL AND UPHILL

I never heard from him or the group again, nor did I want to. All I ever wanted was to be a mom, and it didn't come easy for me. I also wanted to be an Olympic champion. I truly believed I could be both, and no one was going to tell me otherwise. This was one of those moments when I could have given up. But as Brent always says about me, if you really want Jennifer to do something, just tell her she can't and then sit back and watch.

I was now more determined than ever to be at my very best.

11

MOTHER AND BABY

ISABELLA ARRIVED ALMOST six weeks early, on November 13, 2012. In the morning, I was practising my curling delivery on my repaired knee, and later that day I went into labour, making me one of the few people to deliver rocks and a baby on the same day. I was in Ontario, on my last trip to see Brent before the baby came. I was supposed to be flying back to Winnipeg that night. But my back hurt and I wasn't feeling the best, so I decided to change my flight to the next day.

I went to bed that night and woke up 20 minutes later, at 11:00 p.m., because my water broke. If I'd kept my original flight, I would have been in the air, somewhere between Toronto and Winnipeg, when I went into labour. Instead of having Isabella in Winnipeg as planned, off we went to the emergency room at Royal Victoria Hospital, in Barrie. I will admit it took some convincing from Brent to go to the hospital. I can be stubborn at times, and I was scared it was too early. I told him I could wait and give the baby more time. He reminded me that my water

ROCK STAR

had broken, and time wasn't an option no matter how much I thought the baby needed it.

I do believe everything happens for a reason. I was so concerned that Brent would miss the birth of the baby with us living in separate provinces. He was going to come and visit in Winnipeg and be on standby for when I went into labour. But instead, I went into labour early and had Isabella in Barrie, with Brent by my side. I was sad it didn't go as planned, but my doctor and nurses were incredible, and I felt so lucky. Earlier that day I had been phoning doctors in Ontario to see if they would take new patients. And every one of them had said no. Brent had moved so often that he didn't have a local doctor. We had decided that Ontario would be our home base long term, and I would go back and forth. Brent's son, Wil, was in Ontario, and we wanted to be as close to him as possible. So we needed a doctor for our baby, but everyone said no. After Isabella was born I was asked who her doctor would be, and I broke down in tears and said we didn't have one. The doctor who was on call and doing rounds was a family doctor—and he immediately said he'd take me and my family on as patients. I will be forever grateful to Dr. Brent Elsey and his wife, Catherine, who is a nurse practitioner.

Filling out the discharge papers is a moment I will never forget. I, of course, had a Manitoba address. It was where I was living and working. Brent was living and working in Ontario, so he had an Ontario address. We each needed to live in our home provinces to fulfill, in my opinion, the archaic residency rules for our curling teams. We all had to live in the same province to play on a team together. This rule may have made sense when it

MOTHER AND BABY

was originally introduced, years before people started travelling with frequency. But that was not the case in 2012. I remembered the discharge nurse looking at me and saying, "So you don't live together or even in the same province?" "No, we don't," I replied, with a tear running down my face. "We aren't allowed." I love traditions, but I am also progressive enough to know when some don't make sense and are actually impeding change. We must all evolve and use common sense for what is right.

Brent was supposed to compete that weekend at a Grand Slam event in Brantford, Ontario, a few hours from where he lived. He asked me if he should stay, but I told him he should go and curl. He couldn't let his team down, and I was OK. He reluctantly agreed but wanted to make sure everything was set up before he left. Madness ensued as he raced to get things in place. He did everything from setting up rocking chairs to installing the car seat to making sure we had enough diapers at home. He should have spent a little bit more time on the rocking chair because it collapsed the first time I sat on it. Brent has many skills, but being handy isn't one of them.

In came my mom and off went Brent, 36 hours after Isabella's arrival. It was just the three girls now. After a few days at home watching curling—not only was Brent playing, but my own team as well—I felt strong and had managed to get some sleep between Isabella's feedings. So five days after our little girl was born, my mother and I bundled her up into a car seat for her first outing and set off for the curling club. I didn't throw too many rocks that day—I just wanted to get onto the ice and see how I felt. I was hoping I could stay on pace with my return to

ROCK STAR

curling, and this feeler would help. My mother and Isabella, still in her car seat, sat behind the glass and watched. They would do that a lot over the next few years.

This return to the ice was just a small first step, but I wanted to make sure I would be ready to return to action in January. I felt that the stretch in the spring would be important for setting the tone for the fall and the Olympic trials.

I'm sure some people would question why I was on the ice so soon after giving birth, but it was all part of a plan of trying to get to the Olympics. And Isabella was now a part of that plan. Because she came unexpectedly early, we had to tweak our timetable. Brent and I had set things up for what we thought would be the window of her arrival. No one had mid-November in the baby pool. I'd also been through a lot. I had torn up my knee, had it repaired, found out I was pregnant and was now a mother. Life had changed in many ways. With everything settled, I could return to my normal routine, albeit this time with a daughter. I had gone on maternity leave from my full-time job earlier than expected, so I wanted to clean up a few loose ends. But that was in Winnipeg. So when Isabella was 12 days old, off we went on our first flight.

I practised more and more as my body got stronger and as Isabella would allow. In the new year, as I got better at being a mother and stronger on the curling ice, I decided to return to action with the team for the remainder of the season. My first event back was the Continental Cup in January. Kirsten Wall had joined the team in my absence and Kaitlyn had taken over the skipping duties.

There was one major change I made when I got back on the

MOTHER AND BABY

circuit. That was a commitment to Isabella—and to myself—that I would never leave my daughter behind. I didn't want to miss one moment of her life. She would travel with me to every event, no matter how far away. It meant extra planning and packing, not to mention expenses. Every time we showed up at the airport, it was as if we were leaving for six months, not six days. It helped that at most of the tournaments, Brent was playing, too, and we were able to share duties. My mother also came with us to continue in her role of curling grandmother. She was an absolute rock in helping us manage being parents as well as elite curlers. The support she provided was remarkable, looking after Isabella when we were on the ice while cheering us on when she could. I could never have done it without her.

At the first event back, I had a lot of learning to do. One of the most important things was nursing and working out all the timing of when that was going to happen. A game could take up to three hours to play, and that's just the time on the ice. There was a warm-up, an opening ceremony and post-game interviews. From the time I left for the rink to the time I finished my game, it could be four hours. As any nursing mom knows, that is a long time to go between feedings for a young baby. It was uncomfortable for me, and Isabella was hungry. Add to that, the moment I came off the ice at a Scotties, I would have to do media, which further prolonged things. This was expected of us, and sometimes it wasn't realistic. But there was no flexibility on this point—no matter how uncomfortable I was.

In addition to when I had to feed Isabella, I also had to find a place to do it. There was no designated room for breastfeeding mothers, and we were told that our children, including nursing babies, were not allowed in the change rooms. I understand having a child in the room might not be acceptable to all teams, but where were we supposed to go? My mom wasn't even allowed to pass Isabella over the boards to me for a snuggle. No children! At the time we just did as we were told and would try to grab a snuggle when no one was watching. At the Grand Slam events, after a game we could take our babies into the change rooms to nurse, but not at the Scotties or a world championship. Not wanting to ruffle any feathers, I would wait until we got back to the hotel, but I was almost in tears from discomfort. Or if we had back-to-back games, I would go and sit either in a car or in the stands, trying to find a quiet, private place. I remember once nursing Isabella and a fan came up for an autograph and a picture. What could I do?

At the Scotties three years later in Grande Prairie, Alberta, the issue exploded. I didn't have a baby at that time, but several other players were nursing their babies. Once again, no area was cordoned off to allow for some privacy, so the nursing mothers just did it in the locker room. But Curling Canada said that wasn't allowed because of an insurance issue.

The mothers were given some alternative options. The first was that they could go out to the parking lot and sit in a car. One look at the thermometer explained why that wasn't going to work. This was Grande Prairie in February. The second option was to walk to a local curling club that was a block away, where a room would be set up. Or the moms and babies could go and sit in the stands.

I didn't want to make it a big issue, but this was simply

MOTHER AND BABY

wrong on every level. I was angry. It is a basic human right that a mother can nurse her baby. Why were these limitations being imposed? And remember, this was a time when we could play back-to-back games. Sometimes players had only 45 minutes to eat and get ready for the next game, never mind feeding a baby. You don't have time to walk to the neighbouring curling club and sign autographs along the way. I could see these mothers stressed out about where they could nurse. It seemed as if they were expected to go to the stands, feed their child and, oh, maybe sign a few autographs while they were doing it. It was harsh and insensitive.

What made no sense was that in the bowels of the arena there were lounges for volunteers, the TSN crew broadcasting the games and the team looking after the ice conditions. Couldn't a small area in one of these lounges be cordoned off to allow a breastfeeding mother some privacy?

I knew I had to do something, and so after our next game, I pulled aside Melissa Martin, a writer for the *Winnipeg Free Press*, and told her the story of what was going on. I admired Melissa a lot and still do. She writes with passion and believes in equality and fairness. I always felt her articles were impactful, and I agreed with a great deal of what she wrote. I asked her not to quote me or to say I had anything to do with this matter, and she agreed. It was the first and only time I was an anonymous source—a decision I regret to this day. I should have shouted from the rooftops and been an advocate for this issue. Shortly afterward, I saw Melissa interviewing some of the mothers, and the next day the story was big news at the Scotties.

153

ROCK STAR

Curling Canada quickly backtracked, apologized and fixed the issue. An area in the volunteers' lounge was sectioned off for the mothers and their babies. This was six days into the event.

Now every event, whether it's a Grand Slam or a Curling Canada–run event, has a room for mothers. And while they aren't all five-star, they provide the privacy and comfort that a mother and child need. Some issues remain. When I had my second daughter, Skyla, I was told I could use the icemaker's room to nurse her. I thought that would be great. That was until I went in, sat down on the couch and looked around to see pin-ups of naked women plastered on the walls. But at least we had privacy.

It was gratifying to know that the 2024 Olympics in Paris made concessions for parents to see their children in the Olympic Village and allowed access for nursing moms. That's what sport needs, and now children are welcome to the celebrations and to come behind the scenes at the Scotties and Brier. It has taken a long time to get here, but these advances will allow women to have a family and continue to pursue their dreams in sport. What I have come to realize is that raising your hand and asking for something doesn't mean you are weak and need help. It shows strength, and that you advocated for what is right for you and for so many like you.

MY RETURN TO play came with some minor stiffness in my leg, which wasn't a surprise. At first, the leg was a little bit sore, most often after a game or a weekend of games. There was still lots of

MOTHER AND BABY

physio ahead for me and lots of strengthening of my leg. I had been exceptionally diligent in going to my physio appointments and doing all the prescribed exercises. I was also on the ice as much as I could be, gradually increasing the number of rocks I would throw.

I had always considered myself to be a determined person, but this regimen showed a new level of commitment for me because when I injured my knee, I thought my career could be ending. But I wasn't going to let that happen. I pushed myself even harder than I thought I could.

What made me work this hard was that I didn't want to let my team down. We'd put together a plan. We had a goal and a dream. I was part of that, and I wanted to see it through to the end. I was also now a mom and a role model to Isabella, and I wanted to show her that anything is possible. With hard work and determination, we can accomplish anything. And if someone says you can't, instead of shutting down and saying it's too hard, stand up taller and say, "Watch me!"

As well as getting physically ready, I also wanted to get my game back in gear from a mental standpoint. I'd missed a lot of the season and I felt a need to play games, to get my mind thinking about strategy and to work on becoming comfortable with my teammates again.

It didn't take long for us to find our groove. We won the Manitoba provincial final and went off to the 2013 Scotties, where we went through the round robin undefeated with an 11-0 record. Unfortunately, we lost in the final to Rachel Homan.

We managed to make up for that a few weeks later at the last

ROCK STAR

Grand Slam event of the season, the Players' Championship. We knocked off Homan's team in the quarter-final before bowing out ourselves in the semi.

As we ended our season, I was overjoyed with where I was. My knee was repaired and not giving me any problems. Our team was back on track and playing at a high level. The Olympic trials were just a few months away. And, best of all, I was a mother.

I couldn't have asked for anything more.

12

GOING FOR GOLD

AS WE STARTED off the new season in the fall of 2013, everything seemed to be lining up for us and the Olympic trials.

We won two Grand Slam events, the Canad Inns Women's Classic and the Colonial Square Ladies Classic, and made it to the semifinal of a third, the Masters. Those results gave us an incredible boost of confidence toward our main goal. The trials were scheduled to start on December 1, and they were taking place in Winnipeg.

We didn't want to leave anything to chance, so we took some extra steps to make sure we were fully prepared. The host hotel was the Fairmont, and a couple of weeks before the event, we went to the hotel and picked out the rooms we wanted—not just any singles with a king bed, but the exact rooms we would be staying in. We wanted to ensure we'd be away from any elevator noise or banquet rooms and could get proper rest. I even checked in a few days early with Kaitlyn for some extra respite after spending a lot of time with Isabella.

ROCK STAR

We also made sure the food we wanted would be available and picked out some rooms on the floor with a dining lounge reserved for frequent guests. We all loved scrambled eggs for breakfast, and that became our good luck team meal.

One of the more unusual things in the lead-up to that event were the billboards and bus signs all over the city plastered with pictures of us and other curlers. This was part of a promotion to sell tickets, and if our faces had been anywhere else for any other event, I might have felt nervous. But there it was, my face, five stories high, looking out over downtown Winnipeg. Instead, I felt excited. I was finally going to play a major event in my hometown, something I'd never done before.

Playing at home also promised a very supportive cheering section. All of our friends and family were coming. Dawn's best friends from Ottawa flew in, all wearing funny hats so they'd stand out. Lots of people from the St. Vital Curling Club were there, and friends from work. Everybody was supportive and we hadn't even thrown a rock yet.

All this made me feel lucky to have so many people behind us, and the way we were playing gave me lots of confidence. It was almost as if we were living a dream. After the turmoil with the previous team and critics who took shots at me, this was probably the happiest I'd been heading into a curling event. I had a wonderful partner in Brent, the most beautiful daughter, a supportive family and awesome teammates. My heart was full.

That feeling was unusual for the Olympic trials. This competition had always been stressful and high intensity. It was one week that comes every four years—and you had to perform to the best of your ability on every single shot. Janet, our coach,

GOING FOR GOLD

had done a marvellous job of preparing us. We were all locked in on our game plan and knew how we'd approach each opponent. We were a well-oiled machine. All of this meant that when we stepped on the ice, we were truly able to enjoy it.

A few other things put smiles on our faces. Will Ferrell had released a new movie, a sequel to his *Anchorman* hit, and he came to the trials in character to call curling on TSN while promoting his movie. We didn't hear his broadcast until later, but at one point he said, "Of course Jennifer Jones mentioned to me backstage that she thinks they have no chance of winning. She's thrown in the towel." We laughed when we heard about it afterward, and it was fun to be a part of the schtick.

Everything that could go right for us that week went right. When the competition started, we were as relaxed as we'd ever been in an event this big. We were confident in our shots but not to the point of being cocky. We just felt we could make any shot and handle any situation.

We went through the round robin with a 6-1 record, finishing first. That gave us a bye to the final, where we faced Ontario's Sherry Middaugh. In the first end, Jill made an outstanding triple takeout to get us out of trouble, and we blanked. An end later, I made a double takeout to score three, and we never looked back. Those two shots completely changed the momentum of the game. It wasn't that I was certain we were going to win, but we played with such confidence the rest of the way that I never felt we lost control.

For my last shot to seal the victory, I had an open takeout. Even though the crowd was buzzing, I calmly put the broom down for Kaitlyn and headed toward the other end, sweeping

159

ROCK STAR

the ice on the path where my rock would travel to ensure there was no debris. Then I went through my routine. As the rock left my hand, I knew we'd won.

After the tough times we had gone through—from changing the team to the knee injury, the surgery and the long road back—this was the most joyful I'd ever felt in the moments after a curling game. We were going to the Olympics! I couldn't believe it was happening. To make it even more special, I got to hold Isabella and celebrate with her, telling her I hoped I made her proud. She was only a year old, but, oh, how I wanted to make her proud.

The hometown crowd exploded in celebration. The cheers were deafening, and in every corner of the arena the fans were waving flags. I looked up in the stands and I could see my parents, both in tears. After shaking hands with our opponents and hugging my teammates, I went over to my mother and hugged her. All the turmoil I'd gone through and all the nasty things that were written about me over the last four years had taken a toll on her. It was hard for her to read about her daughter being ruthless and cut-throat—and then try to explain it to her friends. But in that moment, it all poured out and she said to me, "I'm so proud of you. We made it to the other side with our heads held high, and it is so worth it." Coming from my mother, who had also made a lot of sacrifices so I could live in this moment, that meant everything to me.

My first indication that this was different from any other championship came at the awards ceremony a few minutes after the last shot had been played. When we stood on the top step of the podium, we were told to take off our jackets and put

GOING FOR GOLD

on our new Team Canada ones. They were red with a big CANADA across the front. It was the first of what would be many pinch-me moments.

Because the men's game wasn't until the next day, we didn't have to go through the meeting with the Curling Canada officials afterward. We did our drug testing and then went over to the Patch to celebrate.

The Patch is the name given to the massive bar that's set up at every men's and women's championship. It gets its name from the Brier Patch and dates back to the 1980s at the men's championship. It goes by different names at other events, but it's generally just called the Patch. At every major curling event, it serves as the meeting spot for fans before, between and after games. It's curling's answer to tailgating. The facility is always big, with room for hundreds and often thousands of curling fans. There's entertainment on a big stage, and over the years some big-name acts have performed. Mostly it's a place for curling fans to gather. In some cases, when teams are mathematically eliminated, they can be found there too.

I have been to the Patch a few times over my career, but I rarely go because I'm focused on curling and because it can be inundated by fans, selfie hunters and autograph seekers— making it next to impossible to do much. I am still an introvert by nature, and as much as I love to interact with fans, I find it overwhelming. But this night, we ended up in the Patch and it was crazy. When we walked in, people wanted to put us up on their shoulders. We went up onstage, where we were introduced and received another big roar from the hometown fans.

I may have been the only person in the room who didn't have

ROCK STAR

a drink, but I was still thinking about what we had accomplished and what we had ahead of us. I was sort of mesmerized by the whole experience. After leaving the stage and talking to friends and people I didn't know, I told Brent I just wanted to go back to the room with him and Isabella and celebrate as a family.

It also wasn't lost on me that Brent was in these same trials as well. His team, skipped by Glenn Howard, didn't do well, and so his dreams were crushed. I let him know I understood that feeling and what it meant to fall short of the goal, but he was so loving and happy for me, aware of our journey to get to this moment and knowing what lay ahead.

Not long after we returned to the hotel, the rest of the team arrived and we all sat in my room and watched the replay of the final game on TSN. At several points we said to each other, "I think we win this game."

As the high of the day started to wear off, I realized how exhausted I was. This feeling of fatigue is something that happens at the end of the week of every major event. When you win, it's even more extreme because you feel the high of victory and the enjoyment of the celebration. Then, suddenly, your body tells you that you've been going pretty hard and maybe it's time for a rest. I don't know about other teams, but it doesn't take long for fatigue to set in and the need for sleep to take over. You put your heart and soul into being successful, and it's worth every ounce of energy. But I'm not sure I even realized the toll that competing can take on your body and your mind.

The next day we went back to the rink and watched the Brad Jacobs team win the men's side of the event. They would make for great partners at the Olympics. Then it was on to the meeting with Curling Canada and Canadian Olympic officials about the next steps, a meeting unlike any of the previous ones we'd had following a national championship win. Its main thrust was about all the things that could go wrong: everything from Russia invading Ukraine during the Games to our not having electricity or running water. They also told us that sightseeing had to be limited. It was best not to go outside the village or get on the subway.

The biggest gut punch, however, came when they told our families it was best not to join us in Sochi—for safety reasons. My parents had never missed a big curling event in my career, and they were key to my getting to the Olympics. Now they were told it was best if they stayed home.

One day ago, we were on top of the world. Now we were being bombarded with grim warnings and stern directives that just burst our bubble. At one point, I stopped the meeting.

"Do we get to wear clothing with the Olympic rings and 'Canada' on them?" I asked, hoping to get some happy news. The answer was yes. So I told them, "Then we're all good." Deep down, I knew there was no way anyone was going to keep my parents and Brent away from Sochi.

Our families decided to ignore the officials' advice and made plans to go to the Games. After everything they'd been through in following our paths and lending support, they weren't going to miss the biggest event of our careers.

The next major question was whether to bring Isabella. I had stopped nursing because I knew there was no option for nursing mothers at the Olympics. That decision was made for me. I was also encouraged not to bring Isabella because she would be a distraction. I felt exhausted trying to explain that having her with me was less distracting because I knew she was OK and loved. Yes, off the ice all I wanted was to see Isabella and have a snuggle. But on the ice, I focused 100 percent on what I was trying to do. Alas, it was an unpopular explanation, though at that point in my curling career I was OK with unpopular.

After much debate, Brent and I decided to leave Isabella in Canada. There were safety concerns, it was complicated to travel to Russia and I was told it would be very difficult, if not impossible, for me to leave the Athletes' Village to see her. I was heartbroken. But I also knew that as her mom, I had to put my daughter first, and having Isabella stay in Canada seemed the best option for her. It was my first of many mom sacrifices.

The first trip after our win wasn't to Russia. It was to Banff, Alberta, where we joined other Canadian Olympic athletes. It was a way to celebrate being on Team Canada and to appreciate that all these athletes had accomplished what we had, but in their disciplines. There were skaters and bobsledders and skiers from all parts of the country. Everyone was realizing their dreams, just as we were.

Then we went off to pre-Olympic staging, which was a pit stop in Europe for a few days before heading to our destination in Russia. This was where we received instructions on everything from getting to our rooms at the Olympic Village to how to watch other Canadian athletes in their events. It was also a last rest period, away from the media, before we began competing and the chance for some last-minute training. The Canadian athletes were doing their staging at a couple of different locations. We were doing ours in Lucerne, Switzerland, one of my favourite

GOING FOR GOLD

places in the world. Lucerne is beautiful and tranquil, the perfect place to get ready to play the biggest event of our lives. My expectation was that our flight would go from Toronto to Zurich. Instead, we made a stop in Istanbul. We all saw that as an omen—Istanbul was the destination of our first team trip after Kaitlyn had joined us.

In Lucerne, we trained at a local curling club for a few days. We also played a couple of games against the Russian men's team, which was good to give us some reps, keep our competitive juices flowing and ensure all parts of our game were working. And then it was on to Sochi.

Before we left for Sochi, we talked about how we would handle everything if all the warnings we'd been given were true. What if our apartment wasn't ready? What if the curling rink was miles away? What if the food wasn't up to par? We decided that no matter what happened, it was going to be perfect. We were going to accept our time in Sochi as perfect, enjoy ourselves no matter what and focus on the fact that we were at the Olympics.

We arrived at our location with low expectations, but it quickly appeared that our officials' gloomy descriptions were overblown. The village of Sochi was spectacular. And as for the Olympics, all the venues were within walking distance. We went into our apartment expecting the worst, but everything was fine. There may have been a door missing, but we had electricity and running water. From the window in our living room, we could look out over the Black Sea and see dolphins jumping out of the water. From my bedroom window, I could see the hockey facility, and the score of the game in play was projected on the roof in lights. We were also close to the curling rink. We could leave our apartment and walk to our dressing room at the curling venue in 15 minutes. It was perfect. It almost felt like Disney World with the various venues and apartments for the competing nations, all within this one area.

Most of the food was tasteless, but with McDonald's as a sponsor of the Games, there was the fallback of an Egg McMuffin, which was always available.

Before we had left Canada, we were told not to pack too many clothes. We were all a little nervous because we'd be away for quite a stretch, and it would be a bit awkward if we found ourselves running out. There would be lots of Team Canada gear waiting for us in Sochi, we were promised. They weren't kidding. When we arrived, we were told to go to the Canadian headquarters for what was called a "fitting." It was like Christmas morning. We received so many different pieces, some to be worn only in certain situations like the opening ceremony or a medal presentation. For much of the next two weeks, we lived in sweats or our curling gear, all adorned with "Canada" and the Olympic rings. They may not have fit like a glove, but they were perfect.

Our goal was to win a medal, but we also had another goal, and that was to make sure we enjoyed the experience. We had a team demeanour about us that showed how much fun we were having, whether we were on the ice practising or walking in the village. Some of our fellow Canadian athletes commented about how happy we looked. We went to other events such as figure skating and hockey and cheered on our teammates. We wanted to take it all in.

We did a press conference ahead of our first game, and it was much more formal than we were used to. The athletes sat at

GOING FOR GOLD

a big table, and the press were seated in front of them. Other athletes recognized us as frequently as we recognized them. I don't think we gave ourselves as much credit for our success (and for our notoriety). Some of the hockey players were fans. We were told that during our season, curling games are on in NHL teams' dressing rooms.

Brent had given me a Team Canada hockey jersey with the number 14 (for 2014) and SOCHI on the name bar, and I tried to get as many Canadian athletes as I could to sign it. Scott Moir, one of my favourite human beings, helped me get signatures from all the figure skaters, and then I ran into Jonathan Toews, who was from Winnipeg. He also loved the idea and got all of the Team Canada hockey players to sign the jersey.

Another day I was walking in the village and I saw a man dressed in the Canadian outfit. I didn't recognize him as he came up to me, saying, "You have that look in your eye. Don't lose it."

That man was Mike Babcock, the coach of the men's hockey team, who was also a big fan of curling. He told us he could see the magic. As long as we kept that look in our eyes, we would win. He was right.

When we walked into the curling facility for the first time, I was in awe. This was a building specifically constructed for curling at the Olympics, and it was spectacular. I remember stepping into the hack for the first time and sliding out across the Olympic rings in the ice. "Thank you," I said out loud. At that moment, I told myself to be grateful, no matter what happens. *It took a lot of time and hard work to get here. Enjoy it no matter what happens.*

Time-wise, the competition was far less intense than we

ROCK STAR

were used to, with only one game a day. That was good because I had an injury I'd kept secret. During the trials, I had a sore leg, which I didn't think too much of at first. But it began to bother me more and more as the week went on. Once the event was over, I had it checked and found out it was a stress fracture.

Every day after the trials I went to physio, where they hooked me up to some machine that was designed just for fixing this problem. I was told I had to try to stay off my leg as much as possible, and even instructed not to march in the opening ceremony. I said that wasn't going to happen: "Come to the Olympics and not be a part of the opening ceremony? Not a chance." So they made me swear that I would sit down at every opportunity.

Easier said than done. The teams from all the countries line up about two hours before marching into the stadium, and so there I was with all the other Canadian athletes, waiting—and standing—before heading into the opening ceremony. Once inside and after we'd found our spot, I did sit down at times, but probably not for as long as the physios would have liked.

Each day at the rink, the physios and masseuses worked on us (I wasn't the only one suffering from some physical problem), and it was a great luxury to have them there. That's not something we usually get at other top events, unless you bring one along. Their work helped tremendously, and I didn't feel out of sorts in any way during our games.

We started the competition on a roll, winning our first three games by scores of 9–2, 9–3 and 9–6. We went through the round robin undefeated and were curling extremely well, collectively the best of our careers. Following the round robin, we advanced

GOING FOR GOLD

to the semifinal ranked first. I went back to my room that night and tried to digest everything. I was homesick but living the dream and trying to stay in the moment. That is when I got one of the best surprises of my life.

I received an email from Jennifer Hall, a Barrie photographer I had recently met when she took baby pictures of Isabella. Jenn was inspired by what I was doing, but she knew how hard it was for me to leave Isabella at home in Canada. She arranged to take pictures of my family back in Canada with Isabella and sent them to me in a slide show with the Sarah McLachlan song "Angel" playing. I cried. Who wouldn't? It was beautiful and kind and thoughtful. And, mostly, it reminded me that Isabella was with me always and she was part of this Olympic journey. I wanted to make her proud, and I was going to do everything possible to make sure I did just that.

THE SEMIFINAL GAME is one of the biggest at an Olympics. If you win it, you're playing for gold and assured of getting a medal. If you lose it, the best you can achieve is a bronze, and there's the possibility of leaving without a medal. It was easily the most stressful game of my life. We were leading by one and had the benefit of last rock in the final end, but as the end was developing, I could tell I was going to have to draw to the four-foot for us to win. Sure enough, that's what I needed to do.

I'd had great weight all week, but the stakes with this shot were exceptionally high. I had to be perfect to get us to the final. As I made my way down the ice to throw the last shot, I felt that if there'd been a bucket nearby, I would have thrown up in it.

169

ROCK STAR

Once again, I went through my routine: cleaned the rock, rubbed my hand on my leg and threw the stone. Halfway down, Jill and Dawn began to sweep furiously and guided it to a stop right on top of the Olympic rings in the button.

We knew now that we were going home with a medal, which was a relief, but we also realized the big prize was within our grasp. Still, the final seemed less stressful than the semi. I was much calmer than a day earlier.

The final was against Margaretha Sigfridsson and her Swedish team. We didn't play well in the first half of the game. In fact, it was probably our worst five ends of the week. Somehow, we managed to keep the game close. We were still very much in it. At the fifth-end break, Janet, our coach, came out and talked to us, telling us to stay with it and stay focused. When Kaitlyn, Dawn and Jill headed back to their end, I looked at Janet and asked for her opinion.

"I think I've got to simplify it," I said.

"Oh, yeah," she replied with a smile and then turned to go back to her coach's position. She was the best and made me smile when I needed it the most.

I did simplify things in the second half, but it was still an exceptionally close contest. We were leading 4–3 heading to the ninth end. That's when Sigfridsson missed her last rock and we stole two points. When that happened, I knew we'd won the Olympics. At least that's how I felt. There was still another end to play, but I was sure we would close them out. I looked up in the stands, and I could see my mother was already crying. I had to look away because I didn't want to start too.

The final shot was a straightforward takeout. I just had to

GOING FOR GOLD

hit an open Swedish stone, like the shot I made to win the trials. As soon as the rock was on its way, I knew we had won the gold medal. It took about 10 seconds from the time the rock left my hand until it contacted the other stone, and in that short period, everything that had happened to me and to the team over the previous four years flashed through my mind. It was an incredible journey, and it had brought us halfway around the world to these Games, the pinnacle of sport. And we were now Olympic gold medallists.

It was hard to wrap my head around what we had just accomplished. We'd gone through the Olympic Games undefeated—which no other women's team had done before or has done since. The ride to get there, to build the team, to win the trials, to support each other every step of the way was magical. My personal trip from busted knee to surgery to motherhood to the trials to stress fracture to a gold medal was amazing.

I remember sitting in front of the TV, watching so many of our Canadian athletes over the years as they competed and won: swimmer Mark Tewksbury, speed skater Catriona Le May Doan and ice dancers Tessa Virtue and Scott Moir—the list went on. Now we were on that list too.

When the game was over, we went to Canada House to see our families. Both my mother and my father, who never cries, were in tears. The pride they felt had overflowed. I will never forget how they looked and how I felt. I made them proud and as a mother, I could sense their joy and excitement. I also knew I could never have done it without them. Brent came over and gave me the biggest hug and just kept telling me how proud he was and how I did my Jennifer Jones thing. He has told me he is in awe of

ROCK STAR

how I can just find a way to win. Coming from him, a competitor I admire so much and my partner in life, it meant the world. To top the day off, we stayed at Canada House and watched the Canadian women's hockey team come back and win gold as well.

The only downside to that glorious day was that we had to wait two more days to get our medals. It was a bit frustrating, to be honest. On the day we won, there was a short presentation where we received flowers. For the actual medal ceremony, they gave us a list of detailed instructions: when to walk, when to stand still, when to go up on the podium, when to bow down to get your medal, when to turn toward the flag. Yes, quite detailed.

When that medal finally went around my neck, I was in awe. I missed Kaitlyn getting hers because I was wrapped up in looking at mine, hanging around my neck. When we all had our medals, we turned to the flag as "O Canada" began to play. As if on cue, we all began to cry.

To win our gold medals and achieve our dream, we travelled a road that was long and had many twists and turns. We'd set out four years earlier with a goal of winning the gold medal. At that time, it was a dream. Now it was reality. It's hard to believe we did it, but the effort, the commitment and our journey proved once again that anything is possible.

13

TEAM JONES WAY

RETURNING HOME FROM the Olympics, we were all still riding a wave of exuberance even though it had been a few days and we were supremely jet-lagged. When we touched down in Winnipeg, I figured there would be a celebration at the airport, much like we'd had after our Canadian and world championship victories.

But nothing could have prepared us for what was waiting. As we exited the plane, we saw Mounties in full uniform waiting to escort us to the main lobby. Sam Katz, the mayor of Winnipeg, greeted us, and then we headed toward the escalators. Bagpipers started playing the moment I stepped onto the moving staircase, and then a throng of people erupted into cheers and screams. Hundreds of fans, many with flags, had come to celebrate our return. There were friends from the St. Vital Curling Club, from my $20 Club, from work—and many, many more people I didn't know. There were little kids holding signs, some crying as we descended. A swarm of media were waiting to talk to us. One of the local TV stations had even set up a news desk and was broadcasting our arrival live, as if we were royalty.

ROCK STAR

Winnipeggers are hardy people, but all of this took place when it was minus 35 outside. It didn't take long for everyone to break out into a rendition of "O Canada."

When we were on the ice in Sochi, we knew there were lots of supporters back in Canada cheering us on. But until we came down that escalator, we had no idea of what that support looked like and how many people were behind us. We were in a country, halfway around the world, trying to win for Canada. These people were at home watching our games, following our progress and, at least according to some, on the edge of their seats with our every shot. It made our accomplishment even more overwhelming and made us all very proud. It honestly took my breath away. When I stepped on top of the podium in Sochi, it felt like I was taking that step for all of Canada. And now I knew why.

As we waded through the throng, people shared their stories of where they were for the gold medal game. One woman told me she was at Costco and saw it on the televisions. Many had gone to the St. Vital Curling Club to watch and cheer together. My sister, Heather, also my number one fan, would only watch from her bedroom in her pajamas (she is quite superstitious) and set her alarm to watch the games, some of which were in the middle of the night in Canada. CBC reached out to see if they could send a camera over to her house for the final game. Unable to break superstitions and not wanting all of Canada to see her in her PJs, she declined.

A young girl shared her story with us of how she watched the final game and cheered us on and wound up on the front page of the newspaper. She's stayed in touch with us since that day,

TEAM JONES WAY

and whenever I'm at an event in town, she'll come up to me and say hi. It has been fun to see her grow up into an impressive young woman. Hopefully, curling has made an impact on her.

Although we were exhausted, the adrenaline surge of seeing so many friends and fans kept us going. Eventually, after we thanked just about every person who came to see us at the airport, it was time to head for home. Isabella and Brent were back in Ontario, so I was going home with my parents and feeling homesick. I wanted to be in Winnipeg for the celebration and to see my friends and family, but at that moment all I wanted was a hug from Isabella.

The next day, the celebrations ramped up with a few appearances around the city, and as soon as they were over, I was on a flight to see Isabella for the best homecoming of all. On the flight from Winnipeg, I began to wonder what kind of reception she would give me. She was only 15 months old, and I'd been away for three and a half weeks. Would she remember me? If she did, would she be mad at me?

All those worries were put to rest when I exited the luggage area into the main hall of the airport. There were Brent and Isabella, and as soon as my daughter saw me, she broke out into a huge smile. Brent had dressed her all up in Canada garb, complete with a couple of Canadian flags—one in each hand. Isabella began to make her way toward me in the best walk-run a one-year-old could muster, and we had a huge hug. With no offence to any of the other people who congratulated us or the honours we received, that hug was the best welcome home of all. I sat on the floor of the airport with my arms around her and tears running down my face. Fans were surrounding me and taking pictures, but I didn't care. I was completely lost in the feeling of being home.

I stayed in Ontario for a few days, but then I had to head back to Winnipeg for more celebrations, this time with Isabella. The Juno Awards, Canada's celebration of music, were being held in Winnipeg a few weeks after we returned, and the organizers asked our team to be presenters for one of the awards. The Junos!

The award we were to present was called the Fan Choice Award, given to the artist who earned the most votes from the public in online voting. The winner was Justin Bieber, and when we opened the envelope and said his name, you could hear some booing. Right before the awards, Justin Bieber was in a bit of heat in the newspapers and some fans were upset with him. Bieber wasn't there to accept the award, which was disappointing, so we stood there, listening to the boos. I said something about accepting the award on his behalf and then added: "We love you, Winnipeg." Immediately, the boos turned to cheers, which were followed by the crowd chanting our name. And with that, we exited the stage. An incredible moment.

Before that evening, the organizers had asked if we would take part in a video piece made for the event. Our team would take on the Sheepdogs—the great Canadian rock band out of Saskatoon, who would go on to win four Juno Awards—in a curling game. The piece had us, with our gold medals around our necks, playing against them. Lots of funny lines and curling deliveries. When it aired the night of the Junos it received tons of laughs, as intended.

Overall, it was a great experience. We got to put the curling

TEAM JONES WAY

outfits away and dress up for the black-tie event. Our friends at Aevi Boutique in Winnipeg, who supported our team over the years, reached out to do our hair and makeup. We felt like super-stars. We traded our curling shoes for high heels and walked the red carpet. We met so many of Canada's great musicians, some of whose songs were on our playlist and inspired us at the Olympics.

The honours kept coming. Not long after returning home, we were told that the street in front of the St. Vital Curling Club was being renamed Team Jennifer Jones Way. The curling club also had a massive—and I mean massive—mural of our entire team painted on the side of the club. The club was my second home, and to be honoured in this way meant so much to me. The mural was beautiful. I was particularly happy that it included Kirsten Wall, our fifth player, and Janet Arnott, our long-time coach, as they played huge roles in that victory.

A little later, we were honoured at a Winnipeg Jets game, where we dropped the ceremonial puck. Once again, the crowd roared when we were introduced, and again when we walked onto the carpet at centre ice. Later that month, we flew to Toronto, where we joined a contingent of Olympians at a Maple Leafs game. We all walked onto the ice together and received a standing ovation.

When summer hit, we also received honorary jerseys from the Winnipeg Blue Bombers and got to be on the field. I kept saying to myself, *This isn't real life. Who gets to do these things?*

When I got back to Canada after the Olympics, I called Jennifer Hall, the photographer who made my Olympic week by capturing pictures of Isabella and my family back home, to

ROCK STAR

thank her for those photos. Jennifer invited us to come back and do another session, this time as mother and daughter, along with a gold medal (which Isabella put in her mouth, as if it were a soother). To this day, she is the only one I have let bite my medal. Those pictures captured how Isabella was a part of the story, and I will treasure them forever. I felt very grateful and lucky that Jennifer Hall, whom I hardly knew at the time, thought she could help us. And boy, did she ever, when those pictures arrived in Russia.

THE NEXT FEW weeks were filled with honours and recognitions. We did lots of media appearances to talk about winning our gold medals, signed lots of autographs and posed for countless selfies. It was humbling to know so many people were excited by our win.

One thing I learned quickly was that everyone wants to see your medal. When we flew home, I thought about having it framed and hanging it in my house. But that wasn't possible because wherever we'd go, people would ask, "Where's the medal?" Early on, I kept it with me whenever I left the house. I'd run into someone, and once they knew I had the medal with me, they'd want to be in a picture with it.

After the initial wave, I put the medal in a safety despot box, but there'd be requests to have me wear it for some promotional events. I'd have to go to the bank, take it out, then bring it back. Eventually, it just ended up in a dresser drawer. When I've told this story to other medallists, they say the same thing. "It's in the sock drawer." Or "It's underneath my shirts." Very few said

TEAM JONES WAY

it was framed and on the wall. These days, with our win in the past, the medal is safely stored away.

THE CURLING SEASON wasn't over in Canada, but there was no real rush to get back on the ice. We weren't allowed to compete at the Scotties that year. I've never understood this policy. Curling Canada claimed they didn't want playdowns conflicting with Olympic preparations, and there were scheduling conflicts. But Curling Canada controls the schedule and decides when the Scotties is to be played.

For us, it meant there weren't many events left for us to enter. We took the opportunity to recover, both physically and mentally, from our Olympic experience. It had been a long and at times arduous build to the Games, and because we were still riding high in the weeks afterward, we were tired. We used the time to let our win sink in and enjoy the gold medal and all that it represented. It was the moment of a lifetime, and it was worth celebrating.

Our last big competition was the Players' Championship, which was held in the middle of April in Summerside, PEI. Despite the post-Olympics layoff, we were still playing well enough to win the event for a fifth time. The win was like the cherry on top of the best ice cream sundae ever. The Players' was one of my favourite events—the best of the best. To win it one more time, in the same year as winning the Olympics, was truly special.

When we returned home from PEI, it marked the end of a long season. Actually, it was the end of four seasons. That's how

ROCK STAR

long we'd been working toward getting that gold medal. Normally, when the curling schedule came to an end, we'd be planning the following year, setting our schedule and hitting the gym and going for physio to get our bodies in shape. But this year, we gave ourselves some extra time to recover and, especially, to spend with our families, who had sacrificed so much over the years as we worked to make it to the Olympics.

It had been quite a stretch for me outside of winning the gold. I had been through a lot, to say the least. I injured my knee, had surgery on it while I was awake, battled the severe pain and went through aggressive rehab so I could get back on the ice. Most importantly, I got pregnant, had a baby and was now a mother. I was ready for a break. Brent and I had a cottage, and that's where the three of us went to get away from everything and spend much-needed family time.

As the summer progressed, I accepted a number of requests for appearances, which ranged from the predictable to the unusual. Among them, I officially opened the International Plowing Match, a massive agricultural fair held each year in a different part of rural Ontario. That year it was held in Essex County. I had the pleasure of awarding a gold medal to a gentleman named Keith Robinson, who had been plowing at the matches for 65 years. One gold medallist to another!

I attended other fairs, banquets and similar events and genuinely enjoyed myself. I think it's a responsibility of Olympians to come back to Canada and share our experiences with so many who had cheered us on at home. Seeing the smiling faces and knowing you made some people very happy carries a lot of weight. I realize that while only a few people get to win

TEAM JONES WAY

an Olympic medal, the win really touches a lot of people who watch and root for you from afar.

Aside from being together at some of these types of events, our team members didn't see much of one another during the summer. That was normal. Because we spent so much time together in the curling season, we all did our own things in the summer months. We could always pick up the phone and chat, which we did. But summer was when we spent time with our families and friends outside curling.

When summer started to wind down, the team got back to business, planning out the next steps. The first item was a big one: Was everyone prepared for another four-year run at the next Olympics? After every four-year cycle, teams re-evaluate their results and decide whether they feel they're good enough to have a legitimate shot at representing Canada. During this time, teams often play musical chairs. Players move from one team to another, hoping to find the right combination that will have what it takes to win it all. Sometimes a player ends up without a team, or a newcomer comes in and fills a spot. There's an ever-evolving cycle of top curlers.

Our group unanimously wanted to give it another run, as I suspected they would. We were a cohesive bunch and got along great on and off the ice. It was easy to read each other's thoughts and moods. We had the same visions, shared the same goals and were all willing to work hard and have some laughs along the way.

Our team was quite remarkable in many ways, but the most important thing was this unity. We were all supportive of each other to the point that we almost felt like sisters. It's probably

ROCK STAR

the only curling team I've been on where, from the first time we stepped onto the ice, we never had any drama. We respected each other and cared deeply for one another.

Agreeing to continue was a good starting point. I then got everyone together for our first pre-season meeting and I put a question to everyone: "How can we get better?" Yes, we had just achieved what we felt was the highest goal possible in our sport by winning a gold medal and doing it by going undefeated. But instead of being satisfied, I wanted to get better. I wanted the team to get better. Every other curling team wanted what we had achieved and were no doubt working hard to get there. For us to succeed, we had to continue to work hard, innovate and find ways to improve our skills.

This is a lesson I've followed in just about every part of my life. The successful people I know are never satisfied by reaching a goal, even one as lofty as Olympic gold. They set new goals and are always looking for a way to get better, to improve and do more. A runner wants to go faster. A business owner wants to have a better bottom line. A musician wants to play better. There are always new ways to do old things better.

Our plan was spread over the four years, peaking with the next Olympic trials and, hopefully, the Olympics once again. Once you experience the Olympics, you want to get back! It really is incredible. The first year was a little less intense than the following three. Part of our success was knowing you can't be going full speed all the time. There must be down times and even down years. It wasn't that we weren't working on our game or playing in big events, but it was knowing that in the first year

TEAM JONES WAY

of the quadrennial, we would focus more on catching our breath and not worrying as much about results.

We did have one change to our lineup, and that was our coach, Janet Arnott. After a lengthy career as a player and then a coach, she decided that her time in curling would come to an end. She had recently retired from her full-time job and wanted to spend more time travelling and with her family.

That left a big hole to be filled for our team and for me personally. In a way, Janet had been my go-to person on the team. We got along so well that at times, we could just look at each other and we would both know what the other was thinking. Words weren't always necessary; a nod of the head was often enough if I had a question and wanted a reassuring answer. Her guidance was instrumental in a lot of our biggest wins, including the Olympic gold medal. I truly loved her as a coach and as a friend. I knew she would always be in our corner and just a phone call away.

In her place, Wendy Morgan took over. She was also an accomplished coach and had lots of experience at the elite level. When we put together a list of possible coaches who would carry us through until the next trials, her name was at the top and I was thrilled when she said yes. Wendy is one of the kindest people I have ever met, and her leadership added great comfort and value to our team.

We were also still working with Cal Botterill, our beloved sports psychologist. Our sessions with him had become fewer, and that, he told us, was by design. "My job is to make it so that you don't need me anymore," he explained.

ROCK STAR

We'd relied on him a fair bit when Kaitlyn first joined the team, bringing her into the fold and making sure she was comfortable with what Cal was preaching. After that, he'd always say he was just a phone call away.

From time to time, Cal would send me an email and the heading would be: "Who loves to curl?" The message would be simple but powerful: "I don't think anybody loves to curl more than you. And when you remember that you love to curl, there's nobody better than you." At other times, the message would be shorter but just as impactful. "Don't forget to smell the ice," he would write.

He would also do the same thing in reminding me to be a great leader and how I could bring out the best in my team. Most of his messages were short—a sentence or two. Sometimes I'd keep them and reread them at an appropriate time, like before a game or when I was feeling a bit down. They were great reminders and helped me keep things in perspective. Cal is truly one of Canada's greats, and he has had such a positive impact on me and my life. And most importantly, he reminded me to enjoy every second and every little moment that life has to offer.

Our schedule didn't deviate too far from what we'd played in the few previous years except for one event. One day an email came to me inviting our team to curl in Siberia. Yes, Siberia! At first I thought it must be a joke, but it turned out to be real. Eight women's teams from Arctic nations would compete in the town of Norilsk. After some thought, we decided this was a once-in-a-lifetime experience that we just couldn't turn down.

Off we went, flying from Winnipeg to Toronto to Frankfurt to Moscow, where we rested for a day. Then another four hours in the air to Norilsk, which sits 300 kilometres above the Arctic Circle and 12 time zones from Winnipeg. It was a remarkable trip. We were shown around the area, we enjoyed some of the cultural experiences of the locals and, of course, we curled.

Curling has taken me to many different places in the world—Asia, Europe and across North America. I never thought I'd curl in Las Vegas—but we did, at the Continental Cup. Siberia was, hands down, the most unexpected and remarkable destination we've been to.

A LOT OF people have asked me if I had difficulty getting pumped up for the season after winning the Olympics. My answer is always the same: "Why would it be tough?" I love curling. I love competing. I love the feeling of being out on the ice. I love working hard, and I love trying to be better. And that's never changed, even on the day I retired. When I'm on the ice, I'm a competitor. I want to be out there, and there's no place I'd rather be. It doesn't matter if it's the first game of the season or the last. It could be a Christmas bonspiel with my family or the Scotties. It's always the same feeling.

Winning the Olympics was incredible, and I thought that was going to be *the* moment of a lifetime. But the next year came, and then we were present in another moment.

At the start of the season, we played OK, qualifying in Grand Slam events but not winning. We turned things up a notch in the provincial playdowns, going through undefeated and earning our way once again to the Scotties. There, we lost just one game in the round robin and, after two victories in

ROCK STAR

the playoffs, won the Canadian championship. It was our fifth national title, and it felt just as sweet as all the others.

When I went to my first national championship, I was overjoyed just to play in it. Never in my wildest imagination did I ever expect to win one, let alone five. Yet there I was, getting my name on the trophy for a fifth time. Only the great Colleen Jones and her Nova Scotia team had more.

14

THE DREAM TEAM

BUILDING A GREAT team is no easy task. I've found it's the same whether it's sports or business. You try to bring together the most talented people you can find and build cohesiveness among them in various ways. You look for the best people at every position who share your passion and vision. You want each person to have respect for the others and the roles they are filling. And you want them to strive for the same goals. It sounds easy, but getting the perfect lineup is extremely difficult.

Over my years in curling, I've seen plenty of teams that on paper looked to be world-beaters. They were filled with excellent players at their respective positions, but for some reason, they could never find the proper formula to make the overall team successful. On the other hand, teams I thought never had a chance ended up on top of the world. Something about the sum of the parts led them to great success.

The team with whom I won the Olympic gold medal as well as multiple Scotties, a world championship and numerous Grand Slam events fit all the parts perfectly both on the ice and off.

ROCK STAR

I would like to think of it as the best of our era and one of the best of all time. I realize I'm not being totally objective or (humble) in my statement, but our records stand for themselves. There were many great women's teams before us, and there are many who have come after us. I'm certain more will appear as the years go on. But we are proud of what we accomplished and for our role in helping to build and showcase women's curling. We were never satisfied with the status quo and always wanted to push women's curling and female sports to new levels.

So who were we, and why were we so successful? You've read enough about me, so let me share these pages with some incredibly talented and successful women.

Jill Officer and I came a long way from that first time in junior curling when I pulled her behind the Coke machine and asked her to curl with me. She was my longest-running teammate and is a great human being, full of compassion. We were teenagers when we met, and through curling we hit it off. We'd see each other all year long, whether it was on the curling ice or just hanging out in the summer with curling friends. In many ways, the relationship I've had with Jill is as if she were my sister. She is someone who will always be in my life and someone I can count on no matter the situation or time of year. I know she feels the same way. This is a bonding that was built through our mutual love of curling but grew far beyond that.

We spent lots of time at each other's houses, and whenever I was at her place, I called her parents Mr. and Mrs. Officer. That's just what we did back then. Even when we were older, they would ask me to call them Leslie and John. I would respond

THE DREAM TEAM

that it wasn't changing; they were always going to be Mr. and Mrs. O to me.

Leslie—I mean, Mrs. Officer—was an amazing cook and baker, and we started a tradition before every provincial. We would go to their house and Jill's mom would make us her superb spaghetti dinner, and we would get inspired by watching the movie *The Cutting Edge*. Mrs. O would also make coffee cake and cookies to bring on the road—sometimes both—before big games, and she even did so at the Olympics. When I got married, her gift was a collection of her favourite recipes. I will treasure them always.

Because Jill and I spent time together and curled together for so many years, her parents became exceptionally close to me. They were there for monumental moments in my life, and not just those on the curling ice. Even though we haven't seen each other much in recent years, I know that if we got together today, we would pick up as if we had seen each other the day before.

On the ice, Jill was an avid learner, a player who wanted to soak in as much information as possible. In junior, her body was so low to the ice during her delivery that it seemed as if she were hiding behind the rock. Our coach at the time, Lyle Hudson, worked with her and completely changed it. He told her that to be better, this change was necessary. Some players may have taken offence to something such as that, but Jill just soaked it in and listened to Lyle's words on why she needed to change her slide. She was like a sponge, absorbing what he said. I remember watching her slide, over and over and over again, until the new delivery became second nature.

ROCK STAR

This story exemplifies Jill's desire to improve in all facets of her life. Out of all my teammates, she is the most open to conversation and is always happy to talk. That was very different from me when we first joined forces, but gradually, by watching and listening to Jill, I became better at speaking out, sharing my ideas and listening to everyone else's.

Jill wanted to talk about everything, and she had no fear of expressing her feelings and trying to get through to others to resolve tricky issues. She was open to constructive feedback—more receptive than anyone else I've met. She constantly reassessed herself and self-reflected to evolve and become a better person on every level. I've always admired her for that. It is a skill everyone wants, but not many have the strength to succeed.

Over the years, if I ever had a curling issue or a life problem, Jill would be there for support. She would always try to solve a problem rather than allow it to linger, something I wasn't good at but learned by watching and listening to Jill.

As a curler, Jill was an exceptional hitter—an important asset for those playing second, especially under the rules at that time. She was a peeling machine. With one great take-out, she could get us out of trouble and put us in control of an end.

Jill will tell you that while her hits shined, her draw game wasn't as strong, at least not in the early days of our team. As with anything in Jill's life, if it wasn't her best then she'd work at it, relentlessly. In our early days of playing together, when we were skipped by Karen Porritt, Jill played lead for two years.

THE DREAM TEAM

That position required her to become better at her draw shots. In my opinion, those years of playing lead really turned Jill into an outstanding player.

She was also a strong sweeper and helped many of my last rocks onto the button for a game-winner. Tall and powerful, she wielded a broom about as well as any curler in our era. It was one of our team's great assets at our peak. Again, Jill was good at it because she worked at it. She tried to find the perfect body position for sweeping and the best equipment. At that time, not many curlers practised their sweeping. Jill did.

Coach Hudson was so impressed by Jill's strength with the broom that he nicknamed her Jethro, a moniker that stuck with her through the years (although I have always called her Jilly Bean).

Something else that brought Jill and me together was that we were the travellers on the team. In the early days, Jill and I had more freedom with our schedules than the others. We would often head out a day ahead so we could take in the sights of whatever city we were visiting, especially if it was some exotic destination we'd never been to before.

Over the years, our relationship has never wavered, but we don't see each other as much now. Outside of curling season, Jill and I never spent a lot of time together, but the gap widened when we had children and then when I moved to Ontario. But as I said, we are a lot like sisters. Even though we don't call or message each other as much as we would like, we both know that either of us can pick up the phone and call the other at any time, from anywhere.

ROCK STAR

I REALLY DIDN'T know much about Dawn Askin (now McEwen) before she joined our team other than that she was a tremendous curler. Before playing with us, she had played the second position, so taking over as lead was a new experience. Some club curlers might think the adjustment is not especially difficult, but at the top levels the shots required for the two positions are quite different. In a general sense, leads will throw more guards and draws, while seconds are primarily throwing hits. For Dawn, this was a significant change. We'd seen her play enough that we weren't overly worried that she could handle the transition.

The first event we played with Dawn in the lineup, she didn't miss a shot. That's not hyperbole; she literally did not miss a shot. This was when we started calling her Super D, a nickname that stayed for her entire career. We still call her that today, even though she's retired.

Dawn continued to play at an exceptionally high level, and as she became more comfortable with the team, we got to see the competitive drive that was within her. She was a very hard worker in practice, and the time she put into her training was second to none. A practice would be at its end and Dawn would say, "Just one more rock." And she would do that 20 times, wanting to make sure whatever she was working on was dialed in perfectly. She and I were always the last players to get off the practice ice.

Dawn also took advice well. When we practised together, which was often, she would ask me for technical feedback on what I would see in her delivery and even her sweeping. She'd absorb the feedback and then go right back to work, trying to hone the skill.

THE DREAM TEAM

We'd see another example of her perfectionist mindset when we discussed her shots in some of our pre-game or pre-event meetings. For many leads, the concept of a perfect shot is not that clear. A guard is anything over the hog line and in front of the rings, most would say. Not for Dawn. If we needed a tight guard, one that was only a few inches from the house, she would throw it there. If we needed a guard just over the hog line, that's where it would end up. Her demands extended to the sweeping. In her mind, if the sweepers would bust themselves to get a last-rock draw to the perfect spot in the four-foot, we should keep that same intensity for a first-rock guard. Dawn wanted her shots to be exact, and she wanted the rest of the team to want that as well. It was remarkable just how much of a difference the perfect guard made in setting up the rest of the end. As a team we had a mindset that every single shot of the game deserved the same amount of effort and precision.

How good did all Dawn's work and her frame of mind make her? In my mind, Dawn is the best draw player to ever step on the ice. And that opinion is backed up by the scoring percentages given at every game in major events. Statisticians will give a player marks for every shot of the game and deliver a total percentage at the end of it. Dawn threw more 100 percent games—100 percent is a perfect game and a rare occurrence—and games scored in the high 90s than any player I've known.

Dawn's attitude when she saw her score was to challenge it. Not that it was too low but that it shouldn't be so high. If a rock was called to be in the four-foot and it ended up only half in the four-foot, then it shouldn't get full marks. That's how she felt. Most of the scoring is done by volunteers who aren't as savvy

ROCK STAR

with the strategy of elite players, so there can be some question marks. As I've mentioned before, I don't believe in percentages unless they're done by our coach. (What really matters are the shots you make when they are needed the most.) Statistics can be pretty arbitrary. And in the biggest games, Dawn usually threw her best. As an example, in the gold medal game at the Olympics in Sochi, the biggest of her career, she shot 99 percent.

Dawn was also the organizer on our team. She booked all the hotels, sent in our entries, ordered our uniforms and arranged for us to get brooms. If something needed to go from one side of the city to the other, Dawn was always the driver who delivered it. Thanks to Dawn, the rest of us had a lot less work to do.

All this may sound as if Dawn is a bit of a serious, all-business type of individual. Nothing could be further from the truth. She has a great sense of humour, is self-deprecating and sometimes seems a bit lost in her own thoughts. If something funny is going to happen to one of us, it will be to her.

For example, after a game we were waiting in the car for her. She often took a little longer in the locker room. After a minute or two, when she didn't appear, we called her and asked where she was.

"I'm standing outside the exit, like we agreed," she said. "Where are you?"

The only trouble was, she was at an exit on the opposite side of the rink.

Another time when we were waiting for her, we watched her come out of the rink, walk over to another car and get in. It took a few seconds for her to realize she wasn't in the right vehicle. At one event, Dawn used the bathroom during the fifth-

THE DREAM TEAM

end break. When she returned, a stream of toilet paper, attached to her shoe, trailed behind her. We chuckled and thought about not telling her but quickly agreed that might have been too cruel.

If there was a weird or bizarre situation, it usually involved Dawn. The best part of it all was that no one laughed more at her zany situations than she did. She was secure in herself and couldn't have cared less at these foibles. She didn't worry about what others thought—she was in on the joke too.

Whether she knew it or not, her outlook helped me immeasurably. I was always self-conscious, and I didn't have a great deal of confidence. If I'd been the one with the toilet paper stuck to my shoe, I would have turned beet red and worried for a week about what everyone thought about me. What I saw in Dawn was the ability to make fun of herself, and that taught me I was allowed to do the same. I always tried to be perfect in everything instead of realizing I didn't have to be. Who knows what perfect is, anyway, was the way I began to think. Dawn brought that lightness into my life. I could make fun of myself and realize that everyone was laughing *with* me, not at me.

Of the four of us on the team, Dawn was the fashionista. She always had a great hairstyle, which changed often. Once she showed up with hair that, if on a guy's head, might have been taken for a mullet. She described the style as having a party in the back. She was also the expert on makeup. I was never great with that, so she happily helped me get the proper stuff. She was our team's celebrity newshound. Ask Dawn if you wanted to know what was going on with the Kardashians or which movie stars were getting married or divorced.

Dawn and I talked almost daily. Some of the conversation

was about organizational situations involving the team. Then we'd talk about our recent play and how we could improve our game. Gradually, we'd move to everyday things, most of them having nothing to do with curling. We'd talk about families, babies, the latest snowstorm, sales at our favourite stores— whatever seemed to be top of mind on that day.

Most of all, a call with Dawn would make me feel great. She always brought out the best in me, and I hope I did the same for her. If I was struggling with my emotions or feeling that lack of confidence coming through on a bad day, I would just phone her, and she'd lift my spirits and put some sunshine in my life. I'm not sure if she did this consciously—I think this is just who Dawn is. In many ways, Dawn could make me feel beautiful about myself, both inside and out. She made me believe in myself in a way I never thought possible.

As I was writing this book, I heard Dawn on a podcast telling the host that her life would have been vastly different without me and that I pushed her to be a better player and a better person. I can say that the same is true for me and all the things Dawn brought into my life.

WHEN KAITLYN LAWES joined our team, I wasn't worried one bit about her curling abilities. I'd seen her play and was impressed with her talent, considering, especially, that she'd graduated from junior curling just a few years earlier. She quickly elevated her game into the top levels. She was the real deal. But I wasn't certain how she would fit in on a social level. She was quite a

THE DREAM TEAM

bit younger than the rest of us, and I didn't know if that would cause any problems.

Our minds were put to rest quickly on our first trip to Turkey, ahead of our opening bonspiel. I found her confident but also quick to laugh at herself. She had the ability to be candid about herself and let us in on who she was and how she felt.

Kaitlyn and I were roomies on the road, and we both liked a lot of the same things. We liked the room to be dark, so we'd pull the shades as soon as we got in. We both liked to take naps. In fact, we loved to get as much sleep as possible. In the other room, Jill and Dawn liked to get up early, well before a game. Kaitlyn and me? We wouldn't get up until it was absolutely necessary. If we had a nine o'clock game, we'd often wake up 20 or 25 minutes before we had to leave for the curling rink. Quick shower, into the curling clothes, eat breakfast while doing all of this, then head to the rink.

We also loved the same TV shows, and we had one rule about them: No cheating. Once we picked out a series, we were allowed to watch an episode only when we were together. To this day, I have one episode remaining on a series that we chose, and I refuse to watch it until Kaitlyn and I get together.

On the ice, Kaitlyn was always supportive, and it often felt as if we were on the same page. If I missed a shot, I'd come down to the other end and she'd put her hand on my back. We didn't have to say anything because that hand was her way of telling me not to worry. As soon as I felt that hand, I knew she was saying, "Don't worry, Skipper. We have you."

Kaitlyn was an incredible shot-maker and a tremendous precision hitter. She was also a great sweeper—our own Energizer Bunny. She put so much effort into sweeping that she would continue to sweep until after the rock had stopped. That impressed me from the very beginning. To me it represented who she was. She had determination and no quit. She would put everything into being the best. I admired that a lot.

Kaitlyn also gave the best hugs. Win or lose. When my dad passed away, Kaitlyn was everything I could have possibly needed. She said and did all the right things and knew when I needed a hug. I loved my roommate of 12 years, and I am so grateful for the time we had together.

Kaitlyn also had a funny side. Our hotel room for a Toronto event had a full-size fridge in it. I'm not sure how the topic came up, but Kaitlyn told us she could fit into the freezer compartment. This was a freezer that was on the top of the fridge in the old, traditional style. It wasn't a side-by-side or big slide-out drawer. It was tiny.

So back and forth the conversation went, with us finally daring her to prove it. In a matter of a few seconds, she opened up the door and climbed inside, easily squeezing her body into the freezer as if she were a contortionist in a magic show. It was beyond impressive.

THERE ARE OTHER people who don't get as much credit for helping to build our team into the success it was. Jennifer Clark-Rouire, or JC as we called her, was our alternate for many of the championships we played. She was along for four of our Scotties wins as well as a world championship title. Although she didn't get to play in too many games over the years, she was a vital part of our team at the biggest of events.

Most alternates, or fifth players, often don't have much of a role on teams. At national and international championships, teams are required to bring them. In some cases, they are there just as a security measure, in case one player gets hurt. But a good fifth can be a huge asset, and that's what Jennifer was for us. She was a member of our team.

Of all the teammates I've had over the years, she may have known me the best. She could tell when I was feeling up and when I was down. Often, when we were standing on the back boards before our game, she'd look at me and say, "You have that sparkle in your eye," meaning I was in the right state for a big game. If she knew I was feeling a bit down after a game, I'd find a note under my hotel door that would say the perfect things to change my mood.

During the week of a big event, if things were bothering me, I'd go to Jennifer's room and vent my frustration or ask her for advice. She always seemed to be able to say the right words and turn things around. I could count on her to set me on the proper path. We wouldn't always talk about curling. Sometimes it was life problems of one sort or another. In many ways, these conversations were an important part of my changing from a shy introvert with a lack of confidence into the confident leader I'd like to think I've become. She helped me get to where I am today.

Jennifer did come in and play a few games with us, both at the Scotties and the world championship. When she stepped onto the ice, she never missed. She was as pure a thrower of the rock as anyone, and we were never afraid of her coming into a game cold.

When she was sitting and watching our games, she was very perceptive about things going on. She might pick up on a particular rock that was curling more than another, or observe that a player on the other team favoured her out-turn more than her in-turn. It was small but very important information that helped us win games.

If there was one regret it was that she wasn't permitted to come to the Olympics with us as our fifth player. The rules for Olympic teams required fifth players to have a certain level of international experience. Jennifer didn't have that, so she had to miss out. If I could turn back time, I would have advocated more on her behalf and demanded that she come with us. (In the end, we did have an excellent fifth player, Kirsten Wall.)

I firmly believe that Jennifer never got the credit she deserved for what she did for our team. She was a key component of everything we did and achieved. Eventually, she parted ways with us as a fifth player to focus on her own success. I missed her terribly.

THE SAME CAN be said for Janet Arnott, our long-time coach. Janet started coaching us in 2007. There was a break when Earle Morris came in to coach for the 2010–11 season, but Janet returned the following year and was a foundation of our run to the Olympics.

Some fans have trouble understanding what a coach does in curling. They may think the players are so much better than

THE DREAM TEAM

any coach, so how could a coach improve their play? With Janet, that surely wasn't the case. She came in with credentials that included three Canadian championships and a world championship title. She knew the game, and she knew what it took to win. In my opinion, having a coach who was a competitive player adds priceless value.

Janet was excellent at knowing us as individuals and as a group. She knew how to connect with us all and how to get her points across. During the off-season, she and I often talked about plans for the coming year—how we could make our team better, what we needed to focus on and how best to plan out the season. When we were in a big event such as a Grand Slam or a Scotties, she and I would talk in her room before and after games, trying to analyze our past contests and look ahead to our next ones.

Janet was perceptive about each of us individually, as well as about our overall teamwork. She was also keen to pick up on successful strategies used by other teams. It was Janet who keyed in on the importance of Dawn's lead shots, and how making them precisely could help us immensely.

During the season, Janet would make up our regular practice plans, focusing on what she'd seen and what she felt we needed to work on. She would also talk with our support team—physiotherapists, trainers, sports psychologists—asking how we were doing and what she should watch for. That took time and dedication.

Janet was also fun to be with. She loved a glass of red wine or two and always brought her own wineglass with her. At one small-town event in the Manitoba playdowns, we stayed at a

ROCK STAR

middle-end hotel, the only place available. We were sitting in the bar area and Janet took out her wineglass, which was made of plastic and quite gaudy. She placed it on the table and was about to fill it. At that moment, Dawn walked in, looked at the glass, assumed it was from the hotel, picked it up and said, "What kind of wineglass is this? It's horrible."

Laughter broke out around the table—Janet's the loudest. And from that day on, the wineglass travelled with us everywhere.

In many ways, Janet was a trailblazer as one of the first female coaches at the top level. At the big competitions, the coaches were almost exclusively male, but Janet never batted an eye. She knew what she was doing and was confident. I don't think she ever got the recognition she deserved for the work she did and the way she inspired other coaches across Canada, especially women.

After we won the gold medal at the Olympics, Janet stepped down from her position. At the same time, she retired from her job at Shoppers Drug Mart. She wanted to spend more time with her husband, Doug, and her nieces and nephews, who were the centre of her life. She also went off to see the world, travelling to destinations she'd always wanted to visit. We kept in touch, and she was always there to chat about curling or life in general.

A few years after she'd stepped away from the game, we met at a Starbucks to catch up. She told me she was loving retirement but had been experiencing back pains. The doctors were trying to diagnose the problem. Not long afterward, I was told it was cancer. She passed away in June 2019.

I miss Janet to this day. I still have her contact in my phone,

THE DREAM TEAM

and I have text messages she sent me that I read when I need some inspiration. She always made me feel special about myself and made me believe I could do anything if I tried. I don't think there's ever been a better curling coach and one whose lessons went beyond the ice.

ELAINE DAGG-JACKSON PLAYED a significant role in my success, personally and for the teams I played on. Elaine is a coach in every fibre of her being. She was ahead of her time in understanding what curlers needed in terms of peak performance, and she passed along all her knowledge to the entire national team program.

Elaine was the team lead when we won the juniors in 1994 and became the national women's team leader when we were winning our Scotties. As national coach of women's curling, she has been at every world and Olympic championship I've competed in. I couldn't imagine what my life would have been like without her. She has been in my corner, made me feel special and supported me throughout my entire curling career, and I will always consider her a close friend. Elaine is one of the few people I instantly trusted, and I have never looked back. Her integrity is unmatched, and that is something we both value above anything else.

THE BEST PART about our team that won Olympic gold was its cohesiveness. We always seemed to be on the same page, whether it was a shot that needed to be thrown, where we

ROCK STAR

should go for dinner or what time we should leave for the airport. All four of us were equal partners in the team, and there was never a hint of jealousy among us. Most of the time we did social things together, but if two of us went out somewhere, the other two were never offended. It was just part of being on the team.

I believe cohesiveness was one of the key components of our success, and it's key to the success of any team. A lot of talented curlers are out there in the world. Talent on the ice can be improved. But it's a rare thing to get four exceptionally talented players together who understand how to join forces and get the best out of each other in the big moments. There is a secret sauce that brings the four players into one unit. I saw that among other teams, too, at the 2010 Olympics, when I was sitting on the media bench. I've seen it with teams I've played against and experienced it with teams I've played for. But I don't think any of those teams had as much of it as our team did.

We used the word "teamness" a lot in our meetings (and, yes, I know that's not a real word) and talked about how, at that time, none of us wanted to play for anyone else. We were there for each other, no matter the situation. We cared for each other, and we just never wanted to let each other down. But we also weren't afraid to miss. If we did, we knew the other three players would be there to support us.

We also had some other unusual components that made us work. The other three said that my yelling of sweeping instructions often got them energized on days when we were flat. If we were having an off game or were just feeling blah, one of them

THE DREAM TEAM

would come down and tell me to yell in my loud voice. That would often switch on the momentum and get them energized. At first, I was a little uncomfortable screaming at the top of my lungs when Dawn or Jill was just throwing an open guard— hardly a shot to win the Scotties. But they wanted it. Most often, this over-the-top screaming happened in morning games, when we were all a little tired. It was their fuel, a way to kick-start the squad and shake off the cobwebs.

The other thing that helped our team click was the authenticity. We are all just regular folks. If you were sitting up in the stands and watching us play, you'd meet the same people at the grocery store the next week. We never thought of ourselves as celebrities or better than anyone else. Among ourselves we were also the same to each other, and we accepted that. I was known for preferring to stay in my room and read a book and not go out late at night. Sometimes the others did, and I had absolutely no problem with that. I wanted them to be who they were, not to fit into some rigid plan that didn't suit them. (We did have a 10-hour curfew rule that we all agreed to. Everyone had to be back in their rooms 10 hours before the time of our next game.)

I believe the most important part of our team's success was the fact we all truly liked each other. Not every team has that feeling of friendship through the four positions. In fact, some very successful teams are more than a little divisive through the ranks. Somehow, they make it work, but I just can't believe it's very much fun.

On our team, I want to win more for my teammates than

for me. I know that sounds like a cliché, but it really isn't. I know my teammates feel the same way for me. In that way, curling has never been about standing on the top podium. It's been about the ride to get there: the wins and the losses, the great shots and the missed ones and all the experiences we enjoyed together. That's really why I curl. Of course, I wanted to win the Olympics, the Scotties, the Slams and every game I played, but that's not what the game is about for me. It's about trusting your team and lifting each other up, about working together and about seeing what you can do together.

If there was a singular focus, for me it was about pushing myself and seeing how far I could go. I liked feeling I was contributing to the evolution of the sport and to the growth of women's curling. I'm proud of what I did, but I'm happiest about what our team achieved.

15

SKYLA'S TURN

WINNING THE 2015 Scotties gave us a great lift at the end of what was really a recovery season. It showed us we were still at the top of our game despite our mediocre play earlier in the year at the Grand Slams. In those events, we'd made it to the semifinal of just one tournament, the Masters, and only to the first qualifying round at the Players'.

No one on the team was alarmed by our results heading into the Canadian championship, but winning it would go a long way in solidifying our belief that we were still heading in the right direction.

As a team we talked openly about the use of social media and agreed we should try not to read anything on it related to curling. Most of it would be good, but the bad could be so destructive that it would have a serious impact on our performance. The trolls can be incredibly mean, from talking about performance on the ice to personal appearance. It was all too much to risk, so we avoided it as much as we could.

ROCK STAR

Next, it was off to the world championship in Sapporo, Japan. Curling in Japan had boomed over the previous 15 years and had a great following, with plenty of fans turning out to watch us play. We were huge celebrities among the curling fans there, and we posed for plenty of selfies and signed endless autographs. We continued our good play, making it all the way to the final before bowing out to the Swiss team skipped by Alina Pätz, when she made a draw to the button to win the world championship. Again, we took satisfaction in our silver medal result and continued to feel the strength of our team, from top to bottom.

We amped things up a bit the following year, playing a few more events and continuing to build toward the 2017 Olympic curling trials. Our play in the Grand Slams improved, and we returned to the Scotties as Team Canada, where we lost in the semifinal. We did close out the year with a win at the Champions Cup, which was a good way to head into the summer.

There was something else coming that summer that was far more important than curling. Brent and I had wanted to expand our family, and in August we welcomed the arrival of our second daughter, Skyla.

People have asked me if we tried to time the birth for the off-season to diminish the amount of time I missed on the ice. The answer is yes, but that's the answer from almost every elite female player (adjusted for the sport, of course). A summer arrival means you can still play while in the early months of a pregnancy, and when the baby arrives, you have plenty of time to get back in shape for the coming season. On the curling circuit, lots of kids have birthday parties in the summer months.

For Brent and me, having a baby at all, let alone planning

SKYLA'S TURN

the arrival date, was a challenge. Although we were now officially married, we still lived in two different places. Brent was in Horseshoe Valley, Ontario, and I was in Winnipeg. Again, the reason was because of residency rules. Our wedding in Mexico had been perfect for our friends and family, who had flown in to celebrate with us. Isabella was our flower girl and wouldn't leave the altar. She held my hand the entire time. It was exactly how I would want it to be, and my heart was exploding with joy.

There were other challenges in expanding our family. One was that Brent and I were both travelling all over for curling competitions. We would see each other at some events, but many of them were either just men's or just women's. When an event featured both men's and women's teams, we had to hope our schedules coordinated so we could spend some time together. When that did happen, there was the matter of the internal clocks, hoping it was the right time of the month. I also wasn't getting any younger, so there was a lot working against us. So planning for a summer birth was not a priority.

We gave ourselves a schedule and said that if it didn't work by that time, maybe it wasn't meant to be. Miraculously, just when we'd almost given up hope, I found myself pregnant. Skyla arrived in August, a little bit earlier than planned, and my heart and family were complete. I had desperately wanted another baby, and I didn't know if it would happen. Joy doesn't begin to describe how I felt. Growing up, my sister was a built-in best friend and cheerleader, and I was excited for Isabella and Skyla to have that bond too.

Of course, Skyla would go through many of the same experiences as her sister—travelling to curling events, being breastfed in odd rooms in the bowels of arenas and learning to cheer on her mom and dad. I always found it interesting that so many fans volunteered to watch our daughters when we were on the ice. Their kindness was incredible, but they were strangers to us. I think people felt like they knew us because they saw us on TV so often and could actually hear our thoughts as we played the game. This is a unique aspect of curling. We wear microphones and do not wear helmets, so fans find us extra recognizable. But I was a mom, and despite their best intentions, I would not leave my children with strangers, even if the fans promised to take great care of the girls. Call me crazy!

THE FOLLOWING SEASON was the last before the 2017 Olympic trials. We played well but not necessarily great, qualifying in the first four Grand Slam events but not making it past the quarter-final in any. At the provincial playdowns, we lost in the semifinal and missed the Scotties. I wasn't aware of this fact at the time, but I was later told it marked the first time since 2004 that I hadn't won a provincial championship in which I'd participated. That record made me proud and gave me a sense of how good and consistent our teams had been. To soften the pain, we went on a team trip to St. Maarten during the Scotties. It was a great consolation prize and we had a terrific time, with husbands, boyfriends and kids joining in the fun.

At the start of the 2016–17 season, we participated in a training session with the national team program and learned about a new philosophy on how to throw the rock. I never wanted to be stubborn, and I always wanted to be better, so I

SKYLA'S TURN

gave it a try. The way to ingrain those changes in my delivery was to slide time and time again, over and over. I'd drill it in with non-stop repetitions. The idea was to use the new delivery without consciously thinking about it. Unfortunately, that never happened. I kept fighting my slide, and the result was that my shots weren't always as good as I hoped. But I kept telling myself I just needed more reps and soon enough my game would return to form.

The fall and winter of 2017 were what we'd been working so hard for. The trials were in December in Ottawa, and in the lead-up we were playing extremely well. We'd won two Grand Slam events and felt early on that season that we were peaking at just the right time. I was still fighting my delivery, although I did have some games where I played exceptionally well at times. But I just couldn't shake the feeling that something was off. I decided I should change back to my old delivery, hoping that would return me to the form I was after. There was just one problem: I couldn't figure out how to do that.

I consulted with a lot of coaches, those on the national team and other highly regarded instructors, about why things felt so off and why I couldn't get back to my old self. I slid out of the hack in front of all sorts of experts, but no one seemed to be able to fix my problem. I can only say that, as the trials approached, I was lacking some confidence.

I felt frustrated that I couldn't make the correction in my slide. I wasn't upset that I'd tried to improve by making the change. That's how you get better. I was merely exasperated that I couldn't make the new slide work and wasn't able to return to the old one. I was caught in the middle.

ROCK STAR

When we arrived in Ottawa, I was determined to get into the right frame of mind for the event. It was the way I'd prepared myself for every big championship. I wanted to believe I loved the ice, and during practice I told myself over and over that the ice was great, that it suited our team and that it was just how we liked it. But for one of the few times in my career, I just couldn't convince myself that was the case. I didn't like the ice, and this time, I wasn't fooling myself that I did.

I struggled from the opening game, although as a team, we played well. We won our first five games but lost our next three to finish in third place. That meant a semifinal matchup against Rachel Homan, which didn't go our way.

The loss was heartbreaking. Once you've been to the Olympics, all you want to do is go back, and we weren't going anywhere except home. All the hard work and effort didn't get us to the Games this time. The Homan rink was playing exceptionally well in those trials, and there was no shame in losing to them. They went into the final and won and were the worthy champions.

While my Olympic dreams were over for another four years, Brent's were not. He played for Kevin Koe's rink, which was a very strong team. It included Ben Hebert and Marc Kennedy, both of them part of Kevin Martin's gold-medal-winning rink from 2010. They played very well in the round robin, losing just a single game. Their 7-1 record put them into the final, where they faced Mike McEwen's team, with the winner going to the Olympics.

For our team, that meant the Battle of the Husbands: Brent, my husband, going up against Mike, Dawn's husband.

This wasn't the first such battle, although Brent and Mike

SKYLA'S TURN

didn't seem to play against each other all that often. Dawn and I had made a pact: We'd always cheer for both husbands unless they were playing each other, as they were doing now. So for this event, I sat with the wives and families of Brent's team, and Dawn was in another part of the arena with Mike's cheering section.

The match was a thriller, with the score tied 6–6 heading to the final end. Koe had the last shot and needed a draw to the four-foot to win. Out of his hands, the rock appeared light—and Brent and Ben, two of the best sweepers in the game, put the brooms to it immediately. As the rock slid down the ice, Isabella and I were in the stands, screaming for them to sweep hard, hoping it would get to the four-foot. Dawn was with her group, wondering if it was going to come up just short. It took every ounce of energy from the sweepers, but the rock made it into the four-foot.

Brent was going to the Olympics in Pyeongchang, South Korea.

Watching him shout with joy and hug his teammates moments after they'd won meant the world to me. I was so happy, it was almost as if I'd won. Brent had done so much in curling: three Brier wins and another six runner-ups, three world championships and countless other big victories. Now he was off to the Olympics.

Just a few minutes after the celebrations died down, I got a call from the Canadian Olympic Committee asking if I would come to Pyeongchang to host some of the corporate clients who would be attending. The job would be to escort some of the top advertisers and backers of the Canadian Olympic program around the Games. We would attend some of the events, walk around the various venues and enjoy dinners together. I would share my experiences of being an Olympian with them and answer any questions they might have. Over the course of the Games, friendships would grow and the group would create strong bonds that would last after we all returned home.

Personally, it was also a great opportunity for putting the first piece of the "our family goes to the Olympics" puzzle together.

There was no doubt that I was going—that was always going to happen, even before the COC's invitation. The question was what would we do with Bella and Skyla. Things got more complicated when our team won the Manitoba playdowns and were headed back to the Scotties in February 2018. That event concluded just five days before the Olympics started. It meant I'd be away from home for about a month, and I didn't want to go that long without seeing my children.

The first step was the Scotties. Both girls were coming, we decided. That wasn't a tough decision because the two of them had been travelling with me almost since they were born. At four, Bella had been to a few Scotties and every other significant event I'd played and had already been on more than 450 flights. Skyla was also becoming a frequent flyer. With lots of help from my mother, we all went off to the Scotties in Penticton, BC.

However, we had a small hurdle to jump over before we threw the first rocks. The Olympics had added mixed doubles to its roster of sports, and most of the top players competed not only in the traditional playdowns but also in the new two-person event. Kaitlyn teamed up with John Morris and

SKYLA'S TURN

ended up winning the right to be Team Canada. They were off to Pyeongchang, where they would eventually claim the gold medal.

For the rest of us, it meant finding a replacement for the Scotties, because the mixed doubles Olympic event started before the Scotties ended. Jill, Dawn and I considered the possibilities and were unanimous on Shannon Birchard, an impressive young player who had a glowing junior career and was now making her mark in the women's ranks. We invited her to join us with the understanding that if we won, she wouldn't come with us to the world championship because Kaitlyn would be back by then.

At 23, Shannon amazed me with her determination. Once we confirmed her as a team member, she took it upon herself to reach out to our coaches and support team to ask how she would best fit in. For example, Cal Botterill, our sports psychologist, told her that when I asked for her opinion, she should be direct and give it and not respond with, "What do you think?" That's exactly what she did, giving me her thoughts on a situation at every request. I was blown away.

Although it was her first Scotties, Shannon had no fear on the ice. She played superbly. The rest of us were pretty good that week, too, and we captured our sixth national title, defeating the Kerri Einarson team in the final. It was an honour to join Colleen Jones and her stellar rink with the record for the most national championships. I didn't really think about it much at the time because I was in the moment and focused on this win, which was special, just as the other five were.

More recently, I've come to appreciate that it's cool to have my name in the record books, joining Colleen. It's something to look back on and feel good about.

That win sent us off to the world championship in North Bay, Ontario, which would come after the Olympics. It added another layer on top of the kids' travel situation, but it truly was a good problem to have.

For the Olympics, Brent and I decided that Skyla would stay home with my mother, and Bella would come with me. However, because I was going to be busy schmoozing with Olympic clients, we would bring along help. So we arranged for Anne Foley and her daughter, Emma, to come with us and watch Bella. I met Anne when she became Bella's Montessori teacher. (She is still known as Teacher Anne in our house.) We instantly became dear friends and family to each other. Anne often helped with the girls overnight when my mom couldn't be there, and both Bella and Skyla loved Anne and her entire family. I don't know what I would have done without her, her husband, Mike, and their daughters, Emma and Amelia. They made Ontario feel like home and like I had friends who'd always be there for me and my family.

When I asked Anne to come to Asia with us, I knew it was a big request and I wasn't sure she'd accept. She began crying before she could give me a verbal reply, and I correctly took that to mean yes. So off the four of us went to South Korea, taking with us enough gear to climb Mount Everest.

All this meant that in Pyeongchang, I was doing three things: hosting COC clients, caring for my daughter and cheering Brent on as he played for Canada. A major balancing act, as usual, but somehow I worked it all out.

SKYLA'S TURN

While I was out with the sponsors, guiding them through the sights and sounds of the Games, Anne, Emma and Bella were taking in events such as freestyle skiing and, of course, curling—to follow Brent. Word got out that I had my daughter with me. My clients all wanted to meet Bella and told me to bring her along. So one evening, we found ourselves on a touring bus as it pulled up to the Athletes' Village. While I guided many clients around the village, Anne, Emma and Bella stayed on the bus with those who weren't interested in the tour.

When I returned, just about everyone told me that Bella had been the entertainment on the bus—and had been incredibly polite to one and all. But my maternal pride didn't last very long. When the others got back on the bus, at an exceptionally quiet moment and in a particularly loud voice, Bella asked, "Who farted?"

Everyone on the bus burst out laughing, including one embarrassed mother.

Guiding the clients gave me another viewpoint of the Olympics, something I hadn't seen from either the athletes' side or my vantage point of the media bench back in 2010. There is nothing that brings people together like the Games. Everyone experiences a shared joy and a celebration of athletic endeavour. That was the power of the Olympics that I experienced.

As an illustration of this prevailing joyous mood, one night Bella and I got stuck on our way back to the hotel after watching Brent at the curling venue. South Koreans were celebrating a holiday, and there were almost no buses or taxis on the roads. As we began the hour-long walk back to the hotel, a wild windstorm hit the area. Stuff was flying all over—trees, garbage,

ROCK STAR

lawn furniture—and we were in the middle of it. A local man approached and took us behind a sheltered area so we wouldn't get hit. He didn't speak English and we didn't speak Korean, but thanks to the translation app on his phone, it was clear he was asking us where we were going. I had a card with the name of our hotel on it, and he told us to get into his car. (As I did, I took a picture of his licence plate and sent it to Brent just in case something happened.) This man was simply a wonderful person who wanted to get us to safety. A moment that likely wouldn't have happened if not for the Olympics.

A FEW DAYS after that experience, we went back to the curling facility to watch Brent play his semifinal match. His team played well during the week and finished second in the round robin. That put them into the semifinal against the United States. Unfortunately, they didn't have their best game and lost, dropping them into the bronze medal match the following day against Switzerland.

We returned to watch that, and sadly, it didn't go well either, as they lost 7–5 and weren't able to win a medal. Watching from the stands, I felt helpless. It was harder to watch that than to be on the ice and experience it first-hand. I was heartbroken. Bella was in tears. Winning an Olympic medal is hard, but I thought the team had played well enough to be on the podium. All their hard work, their training, their sacrifices and dreams of winning a medal fell away so quickly.

Understandably, they were devastated when we saw them later. Brent is still disappointed, but he understands that he

SKYLA'S TURN

feels this way because he cares so much about curling and all that it means to him.

Over time, he was able to realize that being an Olympian is a remarkable experience, medal or not. It's about wearing the team uniform and marching in the opening or closing ceremony, meeting all the other athletes from other sports and everything that goes with the traditions of the Games. So many other curlers would dream of just being where he was, playing on that ice in front of those crowds. It was a journey he made that no one could take away from him.

We have a saying at our house: "If losing didn't make you sad or playing in the big moments didn't make you nervous, then why are you doing it?" In other words, if you didn't love it, didn't have the passion and didn't experience the emotions associated with winning and losing, it probably didn't mean that much to you. We try to focus our time and energy on those things that bring joy, passion and every emotion. We try to feel all the emotions of experiencing and living life to the fullest. It is what we want for our children, and we try to pave the way, so they see it is possible.

NOT LONG AFTER we returned home from South Korea, we were off again to the world championship. Kaitlyn was back from the Olympics, and Shannon accepted our offer to serve as our alternate.

This time, the event was a little closer to home in North Bay, Ontario. For my Ontario family, that meant just a two-hour drive. With such a convenient location, we decided the whole family should make the trip. Everyone came and stayed for the entire event, enjoying what I felt was the best world championship in which I'd played. The entire city of North Bay seemed consumed by the event. We almost couldn't walk out of the hotel without being asked for an autograph or a selfie.

The first day we were there, we asked the front desk where the best place was for breakfast—we were all big breakfast fans—and were told Burger World. Burger World? We repeated that we'd asked about breakfast, not lunch or dinner, but again, Burger World was the answer. So off we went and we soon realized why. The food was amazing. Not long after we sat down, Dan, the owner, came over and, having recognized us, said he was a big fan. He gave us his phone number and said to text anytime we wanted a table, and he'd make sure one was available. That turned out to be gold, because Burger World, which was near the curling rink, almost always had a lineup. We made several visits over the week, the food excellent every time. Best of all, Dan became a good friend.

Whenever I'm back in North Bay, I drop in to visit Dan—another great friendship made through curling.

Isabella even got a bit of the star treatment in North Bay. She had recently been in a commercial created by one of the major curling sponsors. The commercial was shown during every broadcast of every game. She and my in-laws, George and Jane, were out for lunch one day when someone in the restaurant recognized her from the commercial. That stranger was so taken by her that they bought her lunch.

Later, when I heard the story, I asked Isabella why she thought the person had paid for her lunch. "Mom," she replied,

SKYLA'S TURN

"I'm a celebrity too. I'm on TV." In fact, the TV audience often saw her in the crowd or in a commercial we had filmed for our team.

The arena in North Bay was packed every day for every draw. The way it was set up, it felt as if the crowd was just a few feet from the ice. Attendance was amazing, with about 70,000 people coming in for the week. They cheered every great shot for us and the other competitors. When we walked from the locker room to the ice it was along a red carpet, with only a rope separating us from all the spectators. The fans took all sorts of pictures of us—as if they were paparazzi—and they made us feel like we were movie stars at the Oscars.

The cheers were also the loudest I've ever experienced. After every great shot, we thought the arena was rumbling. If the fans were reacting to a great shot, I could shout at someone standing right beside me and they wouldn't hear. The noise level was that loud. It made for a great atmosphere, and it was hard not to get pumped up, knowing most of that crowd was behind us.

We played well that week, going through the round robin undefeated at 12-0. We even got Shannon into a game, when she replaced Kaitlyn for the final two ends of a game in which we had a comfortable lead. Shannon distinguished herself by almost taking a tumble in her first delivery when she used a broom that wasn't hers. She smiled as she always does, lighting up the entire building. Shannon is one of the good ones, and I will always have a place in my heart for her.

In the semifinal we beat the US and then completed our perfect week by knocking off Anna Hasselborg of Sweden in the final. Her team had won the gold medal at the Olympics a few months earlier. It was a close and dramatic final in front of a sellout crowd. We made a shot for two points in the ninth end to take control of the game. The crowd erupted as I had never heard before. It was a game—and a moment—I will not forget.

Winning the world championship was a thrill and another achievement. Coming in a season when we'd missed out on the Olympics, it certainly boosted our team's morale. We also added two more good finishes with a runner-up at the Players' and a semifinal at the Champions Cup to conclude our year.

There was one bigger ending that took place when we wound up the Champions Cup. Jill decided she was going to step away from competitive play. She didn't know if it was forever, but she needed a break. She had told us earlier in the year, so we knew it was her last event. It was great that she could go out with Scotties and world championship wins, a deserving finale if ever there was one.

Jill was a hard worker, a dedicated player, a committed athlete and, above all, a great friend. We'd been through ups and downs over our time together and had always had each other's backs. We'd had great laughs together, been on some amazing adventures and always been there when the other needed a hand or a sympathetic ear. Over the years, we celebrated big victories and lamented some of those key losses. We were teenagers when we started playing together, and now we were wrapping up our careers together as mothers. It would be strange not to see her in the hack or ready to sweep one of our stones, but she was going out on a high note.

Her departure meant an opening to fill, and it didn't take long for us to decide on Jocelyn Peterman. Jocelyn had been

SKYLA'S TURN

on the circuit for several years, winning big events. She had captured the Scotties in 2016, playing with Chelsea Carey. Jill's shoes were big ones to fill, but Jocelyn was more than ready to give it a go.

With the season at an end, *I* was more than ready to put my feet up for a bit, especially considering the last few months of highs and lows on the ice as well as the long stretches of travel. I get asked how I manage to do everything I do and still succeed at the highest levels. After that string of playdowns, Scotties, Olympics, world championship and Grand Slam, with various combinations of kids and family in tow, that question came up a lot—mostly from people who simply shake their heads at the end of the question.

My answer is that, fortunately, I have always had the capacity to take on a lot of things, and when I do, my secret sauce is that I'm able to stay in the moment. If I'm curling in a world championship game, I'm not thinking about the meeting I have the next day. If I'm playing with my girls, I really don't worry about making travel arrangements for the next event. No matter what I'm doing, the world just slows down and everything else goes away.

This mindset did not come naturally to me. I had to work very hard at developing it. Some life experts like to talk about work-life balance, but I go back to something our sports psychologist Cal Botterill once said to me: You need to have harmony in what you do in life. I think of harmony as "being present." When I'm curling, I'm present. When I'm with my kids, I'm present. When I'm having dinner with Brent, I'm present. When I am working, I try to be present and efficient.

ROCK STAR

If I tried to do everything that was on my plate, I'm not sure there *could* be balance. But if I did all that I needed to and wanted to do, I know there would be joy and happiness in my life. That's what I strive for, and thanks to lots of work, I find such harmony most days in my life.

16

THE LONG AND WINDING ROAD TO BEIJING

THE 2018–19 SEASON represented the start of a four-year cycle that would lead to the Olympics, scheduled for Beijing. As we had done in previous quadrennials, we sat down as a team and put together a plan on how we would build to peak at the trials.

Once again, I reached out to all parts of our support team to ask how we could get better. I had my annual call with Gerry Peckham, the director of high performance for Curling Canada, asking what we needed to work on. Over my many years of curling, Gerry was a constant. A confidant who would help in any way he could. I had so much respect for Gerry's curling knowledge but also really respected him as a person. When my dad passed away, it was Gerry's words of wisdom that helped me put everything in perspective and take the next step forward.

We now had Jocelyn Peterman in the fold as well, and we worked to put her into our seamless system of training and preparation. That came easily, and Jocelyn, whose sweeping and rock-throwing talents were already established, was prepared to

ROCK STAR

work hard. We also began working with a new coach. Wendy Morgan had decided to retire, and so we asked Viktor Kjell to take over. Viktor was a Swedish curler who had won the world championship and competed at the Olympics. After retiring from playing the game, he got into coaching and over the years became highly respected for his progressive systems. Viktor took great care in learning how we had worked in the past and figuring out what would help us grow. In my opinion, he is a leader in his field, an invaluable asset for any team or curling program that has him on board. He cares about the athletes, he has passion, he works incredibly hard and he knows how to win. He is a great human being and coach, and I feel lucky to call him my friend.

We had a decent season on the Grand Slam circuit, qualifying for all the events in which we played, and as Team Canada, we had already qualified for the Scotties. Though she'd retired, Jill came back to serve as our alternate at the Canadian championship in Sydney, Nova Scotia, where we went to defend our title. It was nice to have her there for inspiration. Our play, however, wasn't the best, and we missed out on the playoffs after a lacklustre week. I was still struggling technically, and after this event, Viktor and I sat down to figure out how to fix things.

We had one more big event that season, a tournament called the Curling World Cup, a short-lived championship started by the World Curling Federation intended to bring top-level curling to various parts of the world. We went to Beijing and won the event, which was a nice way to finish up the season.

But soon afterward, that joy turned into sorrow. On my way home, I stopped to visit my parents in Winnipeg. We had a good time catching up—they both always wanted updates about the girls as well as my curling adventures and Brent's, at least the few they weren't able to attend.

When the visit ended and I got ready to leave for the airport, wheeling my suitcase through the hallway, I stopped and looked over at my dad. He was sitting in the chair where he always sat, but he appeared to be sad.

"Dad, you know how much I love you, right?" I said to him, which was not something I would often say.

He looked over, smiled and replied, "Oh, honey, I know, and I love you more than that. And I am so proud of you."

I went over, gave him a big hug and left. That was the last time I would ever see him. His final words to me are still in my heart.

A few days after my visit, Dad collapsed at the house. My sister called me as I was getting the girls ready for school. I raced out of the door to catch a flight to Winnipeg, taking only my purse. Before I reached the airport, I got another call saying my dad had passed away. To this day it is the worst day of my life and brings tears to my eyes to think about.

I was so lucky to have him as a father. He was the epitome of a sports dad, a girl dad, what every child wants their dad to be. He would do anything to help his girls, no matter what they were interested in. We had a female dog, so Dad always said he was the lone man in a house of women, but that he wouldn't want it any other way.

Dad got his coaching certifications so he could serve as our coach. He would help us practise, holding the broom at the end of the ice. When my teams began to move into a higher level,

ROCK STAR

he came to me and suggested he step aside so a more qualified coach could take over. But he continued to help out, doing whatever he could to assist us. When I won my first Scotties with that dramatic shot, he gave me the biggest bear hug.

It's safe to say I wouldn't be the curler I am today, or more importantly, the person I am today, without his love and support. It was hard to continue to curl without my dad, without my heart aching for him to be there. I honestly didn't know if I could continue to curl without him. But curling made me feel so close to him, and at the same moment I knew he would want me to continue to do what I loved to do, and what he loved so much.

THE FOLLOWING YEAR again started well, with solid play in most of the events we played. I realized that with everything going on, we really didn't have that team-bonding experience with Jocelyn. The schedule didn't permit a team-building trip to Turkey (as we did when we brought Kaitlyn onto the team), so we thought outside the box and hired Jennifer Kjell (Viktor's wife), who was a life coach, to coach our team on building strong communication and team dynamics. Jennifer was a master at getting us to communicate and finding ways to bring out the best in each other. Pardon the pun, but no stone was being left unturned. She gave us confidence that helped us navigate conversations to be better. Jennifer changed the way we communicated, which made a huge difference in how our team functioned.

We went to provincials feeling pretty good, but Manitoba was becoming exceptionally tough, with Kerri Einarson and her team (which included Shannon Birchard) and also Team Tracy

THE LONG AND WINDING ROAD TO BEIJING

Fleury, who had moved over from Northern Ontario to skip a solid squad.

We ended up losing in the final to Einarson, but our hopes of making it to the Scotties weren't over. Curling Canada decided to give each of the northern territories its own entry. Previously, the three territories played down to send one team, known simply as the Northwest Territories. It was usually a playdown between the best team in the Yukon and another from the Northwest Territories. Nunavut didn't often send a team.

Under the new format, all three would have a spot in the field. That meant an uneven number of entries at 15—the defending champions (Team Canada), 11 provincial reps (with Ontario being split into two) and the three territories—and so a wild card was added. This extra entry was decided by a playdown between the top two teams in the Canadian Team Ranking System—a year-long points race based on each team's performance—that hadn't otherwise qualified. This was my least favourite format that Curling Canada has tried for the Scotties. We had to fly into Moose Jaw, Saskatchewan, which was hosting the Scotties, and play one game, with the winner getting into the national championship. You weren't sure if you'd be playing just one game or playing all week. So it was difficult to coordinate time off work, arrange your family and childcare needs and organize how your family could come to watch. It was, in my opinion, ridiculous. But there were too many points and other benefits associated with competing at the Scotties now, and that meant declining wasn't an option. So off we went.

As it turned out, it was us and the Fleury team. Both teams flew to Moose Jaw for the one-game winner-take-all match.

We ended up beating Tracy and her foursome and became Team Wild Card. We were lucky the tournament was in Moose Jaw, which was an eight-hour drive from Winnipeg; Kaitlyn's mom and my mom made the drive. Like Thelma and Louise, but with a happier ending.

We made it into the playoffs but lost in the semifinal. As we drove home from Saskatchewan, little did we know that in a few weeks, the world would shut down.

In the big picture, curling wasn't a priority when Covid spread around the world and affected so many. But there were impacts that hit curlers. For starters, the women's world championship was set for Prince George, BC, starting March 14. The ice was in at the arena, the television equipment was all set up and most of the teams had arrived. But on March 12, it was cancelled.

Not much was left on the curling calendar for that spring, but whatever was on it, including the Players' Championship, got cancelled. That was just the start. As the next season began, it seemed that things were getting back to normal and a lot of curling clubs opened for play. We decided to add a fifth player to our team, primarily because Dawn had given birth to a daughter over the summer, and with Covid flying around we weren't sure how much she'd want to travel. We figured with five of us, we'd be able to field a team. So Lisa Weagle, an experienced player who played for Rachel Homan for a decade, winning a Scotties and a world championship along the way, came on board.

We flew out to our first event of the season in Edmonton in the fall of 2020, and halfway through it was cancelled. Covid was flaring up again, and our curling season was in jeopardy. Curling clubs in some parts of the country were still open, but they all

THE LONG AND WINDING ROAD TO BEIJING

had strict rules in place about what you could and couldn't do. Even with those, at the very least, it meant there was ice and we could practise. That didn't last long.

Story after story came out that these facilities were prime areas for Covid spreading, and before long, most were all closed again. For competitive curlers, this was a nightmare. There was no place to practise, and we had no idea of when things would reopen. We, like so many others, were left in limbo.

As we moved into the provincial championship season, it was apparent that it would be impossible to hold provincial playdowns. One by one the provinces simply named their representatives to the men's and women's nationals, an arrangement that, understandably, bothered some teams because there was no fair way to do that. We were excited when Curl Manitoba told us we would go to the Canadian championship as the province's team.

That was the good news. The bad news was that we were going to have to make a big commitment to play in it. Curling Canada had gone to great lengths to hold its top national championships with the pandemic going on, taking a page from other sports that had done the same. It created a bubble. All the players, officials and television personnel would come into that bubble, be tested and then, if they were negative, not leave until the event was over. Curling Canada took over the Markin MacPhail Centre in Calgary, which had a hotel just a kilometre away.

When we arrived in what became known as the Calgary Bubble, we were tested and then sent into our own rooms, one person per room, to quarantine for a few days. Then we were tested again. Only after quarantine were we allowed to go to the ice and mingle with our teammates. Outside our rooms—anywhere—we were required to wear a mask. We had to order meals that were delivered to our doors. We could shuttle ourselves back and forth from the hotel in a rental car, but that was the only place we could go. We were allowed to walk in the hotel parking lot for a few minutes every day but were forbidden to enter any of the several fast-food restaurants, even though they were tantalizingly only about 200 metres from the hotel's front door. If we wanted a large double-double, we had to order it from a delivery service.

And when we weren't on the ice, we had to be in our rooms. Most players found this constricting, stuffed into a hotel room most of the day with limited resources outside of a television, a book or the wi-fi. I was actually quite fine with it all. Once again, the introvert in me found this routine almost refreshing. I could huddle up in my room and watch a show, do some work or FaceTime with my family. It was strange, to be sure, but unlike many others who were in the bubble, I found it was a bit of an escape.

There was another good reason to stay inside and abide by the rules. Curling Canada said there would be a two-year suspension to anyone found in violation. Suddenly, that walk over to Tim Hortons wasn't terribly appealing.

When, eventually, we began to play, it was clear we were rusty. Not every team had the restrictions that were in place in Ontario, where I was trying to practise (the residency rules had changed, allowing me to play for Manitoba even though I was living in Ontario). Some jurisdictions allowed curling facilities

THE LONG AND WINDING ROAD TO BEIJING

to open, and some teams were at least able to practise. Inside the rink, it was strange. There were no fans cheering us, and Curling Canada had run a promotion where people could buy large cardboard images of themselves. Those cardboard cut-outs were put into the seats. While the intent may have been good, it gave the arena a very creepy feeling.

It was also eerily quiet. No cheers after big shots, no screams for the home team, no yells of support for a player or province. It certainly didn't feel like a big event. At the same time, it was just great to be playing, to be out and smelling the ice and seeing some other players we'd been apart from for months. Although we played well, we ended up losing in a tiebreaker to Edmonton's Laura Walker.

We left the Calgary Bubble disappointed but glad to be back in action. And a few months later, we did it all again. The bubble remained in place and hosted all of curling's major events: the men's and women's world championships, the Brier, the Canadian mixed doubles and the Grand Slam Players' Championship.

Brent and I came back for the mixed doubles, and then we both played in the Players' Championship. Each time it was the same routine: test, test and test again. I think I had more Covid tests than most anyone else. The back of my nostril felt like a punching bag. Over and over those swabs went deep, and luckily, none of them ever came back positive.

I was willing to put up with all these tests, the movement restrictions, the food deliveries and being shut in a room because of my love for curling. So was everyone else who entered that bubble, although everyone handled it a bit differently. Pulling off all those tournaments was an achievement by Curling Canada and the Grand Slam organizers. It was a miraculous endeavour, one that took a huge number of hours of organization and operation.

BY THE TIME the following curling season arrived, Covid restrictions had eased somewhat but were still affecting us. Many of the top events were cancelled because it just wasn't feasible to play under the strict rules in each location. With the 2021 Olympic trials being held in Saskatoon in late November, the elite teams were scrambling to tune up in as many games as possible. Even training as a team was a challenge. Curling Canada had altered the residency restrictions that were so tight in earlier times, and that meant teams could now be made up of players from different parts of the country, on certain conditions. I'd been living in Ontario while Kaitlyn and Dawn were in Winnipeg. Jocelyn had been living in Winnipeg before Covid but was now spending time with her partner, Brett, in Newfoundland and then Alberta.

That was a welcome change, but it meant our time together was limited. Many curling coaches believe that centralized training, where players are all together in one location, is the single best way to practise. While it's good to be with your teammates, I have never considered this arrangement to be vital. I think that if everyone is doing the work and sticking to the process, teams can still be successful. Many teams have shown this to be the case. And at this point in time, we really didn't have a choice.

It wasn't the best of worlds, but when we got to Saskatoon

THE LONG AND WINDING ROAD TO BEIJING

we knew we were as ready as we could be because we'd all put in the work.

We started the week well, winning our first four games. I began to get a feeling that this was going to be our week. This kind of premonition—where my confidence was soaring and something inside me told me we were going to win—has happened only three or four times in my career.

About halfway through the week, I shared my feeling with Dawn. She said she felt it, too, and that she could sense it from our team and especially from me. She also said the feeling caused her to get a little nervous because going to the Olympics meant she would have to leave her daughter for an extended period.

These are the things mothers go through that most fans might not consider. Going to the Olympics? Great. Leaving my children at home? Very hard, especially when they are young. You can suffer from guilt pangs when faced with these situations. It doesn't mean you don't want to compete; it's just a mother's instinct to be close to her kids.

The week went on, and that feeling I had only seemed to get stronger. We finished second in the round robin and defeated Krista McCarville's team in the semifinal to move on to the final against Team Tracy Fleury.

That game was one of the more memorable ones in my career, thanks in part to something that happened during the fifth-end break. Curling Canada has a mascot named Slider, a person inside a costume with a curling rock for a head. As the break was nearing its end, I headed down to the far end of the ice. Slider was out on the walkway next to our sheet, trying to rev up the audience. He was dancing and swinging the broom

ROCK STAR

he carried. I passed him just as his broom shot out, whacking me right in the knee. I'm certain that his costume restricted his visibility, so of course it was an accident. At first the whack stung, but it didn't amount to anything more than a bruise.

On the ice, both teams played well with a lot of great shots being made through the first nine ends. In the 10th, we found ourselves one down with last rock. We controlled the end, and by the time it came to my last shot, all I needed to do was play a relatively straightforward takeout for us to score two and win. But I threw the rock narrow, and Dawn and Jocelyn started sweeping it the moment it left my hand. It curled just a bit too much, making the hit on the Fleury stone but also rolling too far. We scored only one and were now faced with going to an extra end without last rock.

My heart sank when I saw the result of that shot. I was crushed and felt I'd let my team down. We had a chance to win the game on a somewhat simple shot, and I'd blown it. After a few moments, I gathered myself. I knew I had to get the team together and regroup. Viktor, our coach, came over to me and said without hesitation, "You've got this."

I knew I had to go to my team and show them I was confident we could win. All the lessons I'd learned from Cal about showing confidence flashed before me at that moment. And I wasn't just putting up a brave front. I really did think we were still going to win. We got together and I told the team we still had another end, we still had another chance and we needed to focus on what was ahead, not on what had just happened. Everyone seemed confident, and no one commented on the last shot. They knew we had to be looking to the 11th end.

THE LONG AND WINDING ROAD TO BEIJING

Maybe it was experience or the tenacity that our team had, but in the extra end we threw eight perfect shots. It doesn't happen often in a game, let alone in the extra end of a game that determines who will go to the Olympics. But we played as well as we could. This time, though, Tracy had last shot. We had a rock in the four-foot almost covered by a guard in front. It wasn't an easy shot to get around the guard and remove our stone, and when Tracy let go of the shot, I saw that it was narrow. About halfway down the sheet, I could tell it was going to wreck on the guard. The knowledge that we were going back to the Olympics started exploding inside me. Tracy's shot did hit the guard, leaving us the point we needed to win the game.

The emotional low of thinking I'd lost the game in the 10th end to the high of winning it in the 11th was something I'd never experienced before. One minute, I was thinking my Olympic dreams were over; the next, I was screaming with joy and hugging my teammates. Dawn, Kaitlyn, Lisa and I were headed back to the Olympics. Jocelyn was going for the first time. We had done it. The last two ends were dramatic, but it was more than that. It was about battling through all the roadblocks that Covid put in our way and all the sacrifices our families had made over the past four years. Now we were off to Beijing for a chance at a second gold.

For Jocelyn, there was a double celebration because her partner, Brett Gallant, was on Brad Gushue's team that won the men's side. For Dawn and me, the news wasn't as good. Both our husbands had made it to the trials again—Brent as part of John Epping's team, and Mike, who skipped his own team. They both finished in the middle of the pack, and our families again had to experience the highs and lows of the Olympic dream.

ROCK STAR

Brent remained extremely supportive of me and our entire team. He could say only positive things about how we had played and how we were going to attack the next stage. I will never forget hugging him after we won, and I have a video of our girls celebrating. It was one of the most emotional moments of my curling career. Both girls were old enough to remember this moment forever. That meant more to me than anything else.

For us, heading to the Beijing Olympics was the final step on an incredible journey.

17

THE BEIJING BUBBLE

IN NOVEMBER 2021, when we returned from the four-person Olympic trials in Saskatoon, I had hoped to start preparing for the mixed doubles trials, which were set to be played right before Christmas. As with our event, the winners would be heading to Beijing for the Olympics in February.

I'd originally hoped to be able to pull off the double, with Brent and me playing for Canada in the two-person discipline. However, that wasn't allowed in Canada. If you won the four-person playdowns, you were ineligible for the mixed doubles. The rule made no sense. At the Olympics, the mixed doubles took place before the four-person event, so those who played in both would have a great read on the ice and the rocks in that second event. Canada was putting its teams at a disadvantage by adhering to this rule. Most other countries had no such regulation.

At that point, there was nothing I could do. Brent found another partner and prepared to play in the mixed doubles trials in

ROCK STAR

Portage la Prairie, Manitoba. The girls and I were going to support him and cheer for him, but the family decided first to go to Winnipeg for a Christmas celebration with my family. But then Brent started to feel under the weather, so he stayed behind to make sure he was all right. There were now some concerns that the mixed doubles Olympic trials were not going to happen. A number of players were testing positive for Covid after being at a curling event the week before. Add to that, it was announced that the Chinese had a very strict rule regarding Covid: If we tested positive even a month before the Olympics, it was felt there could still be remnants of the virus inside us, and for that reason we would be denied entry. As a result, the mixed doubles Olympic trials were cancelled, and Curling Canada had to nominate the qualifying team. It was a disaster.

Brent was in Ontario, and the girls and I were in Manitoba. I was sad Brent couldn't be with us but loved him even more for being cautious to protect my dreams. For us, the latest outbreak was frustrating. I wanted to start training for the Games, and I really wanted to get back to Ontario to do that. I could have stayed in Winnipeg and practised, but I didn't have any of my gear—the girls and I were spending just a couple of days to see family and celebrate the holidays.

Curling Canada officials were now involved in how I was going to get home. They didn't want me to fly because they felt that was high risk. Instead, they suggested I drive. I enlightened them that it was a 25-hour trip, and it was the middle of winter through some rural roads where there were no stops for hours. As well, the organization didn't want us sleeping at any hotels. All of which made it next to impossible to drive because

THE BEIJING BUBBLE

we weren't sleeping in our car in the middle of winter. I had my two young daughters with me.

I elected to fly home but only after dressing the kids up in layer after layer of personal protective equipment (PPE). I followed the same dress code, and we walked onto the plane looking as if we were going to the moon rather than Pearson International. I cleaned everything within our reach with wipes and told the girls not to touch anything. It was easily the most scared I'd ever seen them. They didn't even take off their masks to have a drink. The mom in me was so sad they had to experience the reality of the situation. The precautions were necessary because if the kids got sick, it meant I would probably catch something too. First and foremost, I didn't want the kids to catch Covid for obvious reasons. But if I caught it, I wouldn't be heading to the Olympics.

When we got home, Brent was in a 14-day quarantine out of caution and stayed at a hotel. That included over Christmas, so there was no family celebration. It was just me, Isabella and Skyla, and a lot of family and friends having Zoom sessions throughout the day. Everything else was shut down including the schools. So once Christmas ended, I was homeschooling.

I was also trying to put a plan in place for the team to practise together before heading to Beijing. The easiest option seemed to be for me to fly to Winnipeg where the others were and train from there. But the Olympic organizers ruled that every athlete had to get a specialized Covid test before heading to Beijing, and those were available only in Toronto, Vancouver and Calgary. As well, we would be leaving from Toronto, so it ended up making more sense for Kaitlyn, Jocelyn, Dawn and Lisa to be there to

ROCK STAR

practise. That was especially hard for Dawn because it meant extra time away from her kids.

Next, we needed a place to practice. Under the regulations in place in Ontario, all the curling clubs had shut their doors. In fact, some closed up for the rest of the season, letting the ice melt away. I became concerned that we wouldn't have anywhere to train, but we managed to convince the Alliston Curling Club (a couple of hours from Toronto) to keep its facility open just for us. There were strict rules in place, of course. We weren't allowed to have any face-to-face contact with the icemaker, who was the only other person allowed into the club, and we had to pay the expenses of keeping everything open, which wasn't cheap. But we were thankful for what the club did, giving us a place to train. It wasn't ideal, but it was something. And if something came out of that crazy time in the world it was gratitude for what we had.

Finally, we had to find a place to stay. The rules were that our accommodations had to be separate from everyone else's, and we could have no contact with anyone outside our team. We rented an Airbnb that wasn't far from the curling club, but it turned out to be riddled with mice that ran all over during the night. A second place was secured, and we locked ourselves in. The only time we could leave was to go to the curling club. We weren't allowed to go to the grocery store or the coffee shop or anywhere else.

This arrangement was far from ideal as we tried to keep ourselves in top form. Between the rules that were in place at home and the ones we had to follow to make sure we could go to the Olympics, it felt as if we spent most of our energy looking

THE BEIJING BUBBLE

after the logistics of how everything was going to work, affecting not only us but also our families and others back home.

We just didn't feel competition-ready to take on the best teams in the world on sport's biggest stage. We kept hearing people say it was going to be the same for everyone, but that wasn't true. In some countries, there was more freedom and teams were able to play competitive games against others. We were stuck on our own little island and not able to prepare the way we normally would.

When it was time to leave for Beijing, we had more logistics to sort out. If we wanted to be there in time for the opening ceremony, we would need to fly on a plane arranged by the Canadian Olympic Committee for just athletes and officials. That meant leaving Canada several days before the start and not being on the ice for more than a week before our first game. That wasn't going to work.

Our other option, which we went with, was to travel on a later flight that went through one of three different locations Beijing deemed acceptable. Ours went via Zurich. Of course we had to wear lots of PPE, including face shields that made it nearly impossible to sleep.

While much of the spread of the virus had subsided in parts of the world, we were once again headed into a bubble. This one would be far more extreme than what we had experienced in Calgary.

WHEN WE ARRIVED in Beijing, the airport terminal we landed at was shut down except for the Olympians arriving there. Right

ROCK STAR

away, we were required to do two tests. The first was a throat swab, and the second was up the nose. That latter one may have been the deepest nose test I'd ever had. It felt as if the swab was going to knock my eyeball out. I can still feel the discomfort when I think about it. Next, we went to the Athletes' Village, where we were locked in our rooms until our tests showed us to be Covid-free. Tape was stretched across the door so the powers that be could make sure you hadn't left.

Testing became a regular thing. Every morning, before you could leave the Athletes' Village, you had to do a Covid test. Testing positive was about the worst thing that could happen. It meant you would be taken out of the village and into a Chinese hospital for up to three weeks. It also felt as if you were being watched all day, every day. Robots, which travelled wherever competitions took place, wheeled over to warn you if your mask wasn't on properly. All anyone talked about was the fear of testing positive and the strict protocols, thus sucking the joy out of the Olympic experience.

A few days after our arrival and once we'd been declared Covid-free, we went to the curling facility to practise. We saw the other teams, and every discussion seemed to be about how everyone was surviving. When the competition started, it was eerie. Here was this gorgeous arena built just for curling, and it was empty. It was the opposite of what an Olympics should be.

The lack of fans also presented an unusual problem. At most big events, fans in the stands bring with them a lot of moisture, which creates issues on the ice. Massive dehumidifiers are usually needed to keep the ice from getting frosty. In Beijing, organizers

THE BEIJING BUBBLE

had the opposite problem: The arena air was too dry. So big humidifiers were brought in to make the ice surface playable.

While fans weren't allowed to watch the competitions, the athletes could go see their fellow competitors in different events. But travel between the venues was difficult. We were only able to go to events that were close by—figure skating and short- and long-track speed skating. The skiing and sledding events were a long way off, and the protocols made it next to impossible to travel out there to watch.

The food was another issue. My stomach couldn't handle the meals being served in the dining hall, and I was in bad shape for a while. For the first time, McDonald's was no longer a sponsor, so I couldn't fall back on the Egg McMuffins as I did in Sochi. The Canadian Olympic Committee did bring some food over for snacks: cup of soups, crackers and peanut butter—and that's pretty much what I lived on for the entire Olympics. I was hungry the entire time. It also added to the isolation as my team would often head to the dining hall together, but even the smell would make me feel nauseated, so I was always alone. It was the first time in my life that I felt like an outsider on my team . . . I felt so alone. But I almost felt guilty for feeling this way. We were at the Olympics, and it was supposed to be a dream come true.

In addition to all the Covid tests, drug testing still had to be done. Once, when I was in bed, my door was opened and in walked two people dressed in what looked like Hazmat suits. We walked together to testing, I provided a urine sample for them and then I was escorted back to my room. I understand why

ROCK STAR

drug testing is required in sport, but it really is awful and embarrassing. All because people cheat. One of the things I most look forward to after I retire from curling is no more drug testing. Not having to say where I am going to be every day of my life so a tester can randomly show up. No longer having to ask my daughters to delay bedtime or an activity because I need to give a urine sample. No longer having to let strangers in my home and hang out with them for a few hours until I have to pee. I also can't wait to take multivitamins and look after myself like most Canadians do without the fear of testing positive.

The next time I saw the Hazmat guardians was when they escorted some Russian athletes away. The Russians were just across a small green space from us, and there was an outbreak among them. They were put into an ambulance and off they went to who knows where. That sight gave us a sense of dread. *If we test positive, that's going to be us.*

And the problems didn't subside when the competition started. The rock handles, which have a sensor in them that tells when a player has held on to the stone after it crosses the hog line, weren't working. Or at least some weren't working. The officials knew about this and told us at a pre-tournament meeting that if a player throws a rock handle and the green light doesn't go off, it will be deemed a hog-line violation. We were told it was up to us to make sure the rock handle was working before we threw it.

That seemed backward to what should have been happening. It wasn't the curler's responsibility to make sure the equipment was working. That was up to the officials. In our game against Japan, on five occasions my rock failed to work before I threw it.

THE BEIJING BUBBLE

That meant I had to stop, call an official over to be a line judge and then get back in the hack and deliver my stone. It was a massive distraction and extremely frustrating.

We brought the issue to the Olympic officials' attention, trying to explain that these faulty rock handles caused big problems, but nothing changed. The governing body refused to alter what was clearly a significant issue for which they were responsible. The very next draw saw similar problems with the rock handles on the sheet we'd come off. The men complained, and this time the officials capitulated, declaring that the rock handles were no longer in play. Once again, the women were treated differently from the men. I'm not sure if the guys complained louder or were more demanding, but the result was stunning. And to make it worse, I don't believe the officials saw the inequity.

It wasn't a huge surprise to me that, after all we'd been through, when the actual competition started, we weren't at our best. We won our opening game but then lost three in a row, putting us in a difficult position. The team rallied and we managed to finish the week at 5-4, which was good enough for a three-way tie for the last playoff spot. Instead of tiebreakers, however, the Olympics used draw-to-the-button distance. Before each game starts, teams throw two rocks to the button, with the overall distance being measured. The shorter the distance, the higher the ranking. Our distance was third among the three tied teams by centimetres, and so we were eliminated while Japan and the United Kingdom moved on to the playoffs.

It was probably the hardest way to be eliminated I've ever experienced. It wasn't due to a missed shot or a great shot by the

ROCK STAR

other team. It was just having to sit and watch the other teams with better distances move on.

Before I left the ice, I wanted to take a moment just to look at the facility, the ice and the rings and take it all in one last time. I knew this would probably be my last Olympic experience, and so I wanted to say goodbye. Instead, officials rushed me off to talk to the media. Right after that, as I tried to get back to the ice for my farewell, I ran into the Japanese team skipped by Satsuki Fujisawa. They were obviously excited about making the playoffs but seemed even more overjoyed to see me. I had become good friends with them, and they considered me some sort of role model. They each locked me up in a bear hug and were crying, thanking me for all that I'd done. I responded by telling them how proud I was of them and wished them well in their next game. I was humbled by their show of affection and admiration, and having lost, it couldn't have come at a better time.

I asked if I could go back on the ice for one last goodbye and was reluctantly allowed. I told my team what I was doing, and so we all went back on the ice to look around, smell the ice and say farewell to what had been an unusual but still memorable experience. Seeing the ice, with the Olympic rings embedded in it, made me emotional about where my curling career had taken me. That moment has stayed with me.

I was still gutted at not making the playoffs, and I felt we'd let the entire country down. On one side, Canada was a curling powerhouse and now we were coming home without a medal despite all the expectations. But on the other was the fact that we'd had huge hurdles to overcome to make it to the Games, and

THE BEIJING BUBBLE

we were proud of the winding journey we took just to get onto the ice in Beijing.

When I got back to my room, I talked with Brent over Face-Time. He'd experienced that same feeling when his team failed to win a medal and could relate to what I was going through. I told him how crushed I was, and he just kept reinforcing how proud he was of what I'd accomplished. It was great to hear those words, but I was still heartbroken at not bringing home a medal to show Isabella and Skyla.

We couldn't wait to get home and back to some sense of normalcy, including some decent food. When I arrived, my kids also gave me some perspective. Brent dressed the girls from head to toe in Canada gear and met me at the airport. They saw me and came running, and we fell to the ground in the biggest family hug of my life. They were excited to see me, were beyond proud of me and didn't care that I didn't have a medal. I had tried my best. I often think how happy the world would be if we supported each other the way young children do. With no pressures of outcome but focused only on effort and trying our best. Seeing Brent, Isabella and Skyla instantly healed my heart and gave me the perspective I needed. I was proud of us too.

As I reflect, I am proud of what we did in Beijing. But I wish we didn't have such a heavy burden to hold. Every time we were told of another challenge we were to face in preparation or in Beijing, we were reminded to be grateful that we were Olympians. It felt wrong to be sad or upset that the dream wasn't what it should have been. That we couldn't be honest with ourselves and deal with the sense of loss over not getting the full Olympic experience. That we were isolated and alone

ROCK STAR

and couldn't share the experience with our families, who were a massive part of our journey. I do believe in having a positive outlook, but I also believe you can't ignore what is right in front of you. It was hard not to. You wanted to feel elation and joy, and if you didn't it felt like failure. This is not a mindset that leads to success very often.

18

DREAM BIG

WHEN THE OLYMPICS ended, we all took some time to think about our individual futures. Dawn and Kaitlyn and I had curled together for 12 years, which is an exceptionally long time in curling. Jocelyn played with us for four years and Lisa for two years, and they both became an integral part of the team over that period. It had been a great run with lots of success and many memorable times together, both on and off the ice, despite Covid changing the world. I knew I wasn't done, but I wasn't sure I could commit to another four years.

Kaitlyn said she wanted to skip and start a family, which wasn't a surprise in any way. She was going to form a new team, and Jocelyn was going to be a part of it. Dawn was retiring to spend more time with her kids. She'd spent a lot of time on the road with curling, and now she wanted to devote more time to her family. That wasn't hard to understand and something I knew was coming.

Most people thought I should retire to spend more time with my family. I can't even begin to tell you how many times I

251

ROCK STAR

was told I should re-evaluate my priorities and put my kids first. I often wondered how many dads were told they should retire to spend more time with their families. I am guessing none. I had been on the curling circuit for a long time and always felt I'd done a good job of being present for my kids. When they were little, they came everywhere I went: literally every single event. As they got older and started having their own priorities, like school and activities, they stayed home more. But even when I wasn't physically present, I tried to be a part of their lives. I'd leave notes in their lunchboxes and read bedtime stories over FaceTime. I would help them with their homework, and if there was an event of some type going on in their lives, I made sure someone broadcast it for me over FaceTime or Zoom. Their teachers regularly told me that despite all my travel, I was as present as any of the other parents who didn't have my travel schedule—and, in many cases, I was even more present. Being there for my girls was very important to me and took a lot of effort, but it was so worth it.

But I did want to be there more physically too. I wanted to be able to give them a hug and be front-row centre for all the parts of their lives. I wanted to be that mom cheering loud from the stands like my mom was.

However, my heart still needed a bit more time on the ice. Curling had almost been shut down during the pandemic, and I felt as if I never really had a chance to say goodbye to the many places, events and people I'd played over the years. I didn't want a farewell tour; this was just for me to play in the locations and bonspiels I had gone to during my career and do it knowing it

DREAM BIG

would be my last time. I just wanted to be at peace with the end of my career.

I sat down and tried to decide what I wanted to get out of the game for however many more years I would play. I'd spent the last few years navigating through the roadblocks that Covid had put up and trying to get to the Olympics. I hadn't really enjoyed my time as much as I usually did. It wasn't really a grind by any means, but it also wasn't as fun as it had been. I wanted to love the game again and smell the ice at all my favourite stops.

So I called up Karlee Burgess, who played on a young and talented team out of Winnipeg. They'd played in the Scotties the previous two years, and Karlee reminded me of myself at her age. She had a sparkle, and I could see how much she loved the game. I'd first reached out to Karlee a few years earlier to see if she would be our fifth player at the 2021 Scotties played in the bubble in Calgary, but her team qualified to play. Now, having the opportunity to have a brief conversation with her, I knew I would love to play with her.

It was clear she loved the game and that she got a lot of joy from it. I didn't know a lot about the rest of her teammates— Lauren Lenentine and sisters Mackenzie and Emily Zacharias— but they were the up-and-coming team in Canadian curling, and I really thought I could help them gain experience. I thought playing with them would be a perfect final act for my career, to see the game through their eyes and maybe pass on some of my experience and help them take the next steps in their curling careers.

Karlee was over the moon about my proposal and went back to the rest of the team to talk it over. I told her I was fine if they wanted to make it a five-player team. That would allow me to miss the odd event if needed or if there was a conflict with my mixed doubles play with Brent or an event at home. For instance, the first stop on the schedule was the same time as the first day of school for my kids, and I didn't want to miss that.

I told the team it would be for a year or maybe two. After that, I would reassess where I wanted to be with curling. For me, this arrangement was perfect. I was excited to be able to mentor these young players and leave curling the way I started it, with a complete love for the game.

As we started to prepare for the next season, my relationship with the players grew. We shared views on lots of topics in addition to curling. They all took a liking to Skyla and Isabella, with Karlee really connecting with Skyla, who would send Karlee messages as if she were a best friend. I talked a lot with Lauren, our team organizer who entered events and booked our travel arrangements. And our calls weren't always about curling. We chatted about various topics, and we still connect with each other. Lauren reminds me a lot of me. She is hard-working, she's determined and she wants to be the best at her position. She has the sparkle for everything in life.

When I thought about these friendships it seemed a little unusual considering I was roughly the same age as these girls' parents. They were all still in school, mixing their studies with competitive curling, just as I had done. They didn't remind me of most people who were their age though. They clearly had

DREAM BIG

goals and were driven to reach them. Again, it was the same way I'd approached things when I was their age.

When we sat down to plan out the year, they told me they wanted me to always be honest with them. They wanted me to tell them what they needed to do to be better. I did that, and the first thing I told them was that they were going to have to put more work into it: "You're going to have to practise more, and it's going to take an everyday commitment to reach our goals. Curling will need to become your priority; it's going to trump pretty much everything else in your life." I don't think they were surprised by anything I said, and I'm sure they thought they were already putting in a lot of work. Indeed, they were. But now it was time to turn it up a notch.

Our practices went really, really well and that translated into great results as the season started. We played well in the early events, making it to the playoffs in almost every tournament. I was very happy with the way I was playing, and I knew that competing with these young women was re-energizing me. They were very supportive and believed I was going to make every shot. They had complete confidence in me whenever I stepped into the hack to throw my rock. Even when I missed, they were right there, telling me we'd make the next one. It was a good feeling to know they had my back.

If there were any surprises in the early going, it was that I called for them to play a lot more draws than they were used to. Young teams usually rely more on hits than draws, so I wasn't shocked by their reaction. At our first practice, I told them they were going to have to get better at playing draws because that's

255

ROCK STAR

how the top teams win. I knew they just weren't as consistent as they needed to be. So in our first few events, I called for them to play a lot of draws to the point where I think it was almost uncomfortable for them. It was an aggressive strategy, and we didn't play that way for long, but I wanted to show them why it was so important to have these shots in our arsenal.

It didn't take them long to improve this part of their game. They worked hard on it, and the results started to show in big matches. They began to trust their ability to make draws at key points of ends, and that led to a lot more wins for us.

Viktor Kjell was coaching us at the start of the season, but we parted ways with him when he received an offer to coach the Swiss national team. I was very happy to see him get this great position, but it was also tough to see him go. I've had a lot of great coaches over the years, and there's little doubt that he was the best technical coach I ever had as well as someone who could restore my confidence during down moments in big games. I'm not sure we would have accomplished all we did if he hadn't been with us over the previous four years.

In his place, we brought in Glenn Howard as our coach. He was one of the most successful players in the sport's history, and to have him helping us out was a huge bonus. He had so much energy, offered up so much great advice and wasn't afraid to tell us what we needed to know. Glenn is an extraordinary person and teammate, and he excelled at reminding us that the team always comes first. That's how he lives his curling life and why he's curled for so long. It's the sense of team, and he was instilling that in us. The most difficult part for Glenn coaching us was that he had to wear a Team Manitoba jacket, a giant step to make for

DREAM BIG

a lifelong Ontario curler. We threw lots of laughs and fun jabs his way when we'd see him sporting the western province's colours and the Buffalo emblem on his back.

Our season had started on a high note. We won the season opener, the Saville Shootout, going undefeated. At the next event, the PointsBet Invitational, our hot streak continued, and we won that without a loss.

When the provincial playdowns rolled around, we were hitting our stride, and we won the Manitoba championship, again going undefeated. We took that momentum into the Canadian championship, which was in Kamloops, BC, and felt good about our chances.

Although the other four players had been in the Scotties the two previous years, they still possessed a sense of excitement and wonder at being at the event. I could see it in their eyes and hear it in their voices when we first got to the arena, and I was reminded of my early days at the Scotties. Their enthusiasm really energized me.

All that spirit showed when we got rolling as we went through the round robin with just a single loss, and I think our performance surprised a lot of people who believed we had just been lucky with our season and our play at the Scotties. There were comments that "Jennifer and the Kids," as one report called us, weren't ready to win a national championship. And how could they do it with a five-person team, rotating players in and out of the lineup?

But we believed. We knew. As far as we were concerned, we were as good as any team in the event. We won the first playoff game, which sent us into the final against the defending champions skipped by Kerri Einarson. That game didn't go our way, and it was heartbreaking not to win after getting so close. I felt for the other four, and it wasn't hard to see the disappointment in their faces. I told them how proud I was of them all and that to reach this level in our first year together was an achievement we needed to soak up. We weren't going to win every game and certainly not every big game, but this is why we played: to get these experiences and to feel the excitement and the thrill of playing in a Canadian championship. I reminded them of my saying, "If we knew we were going to win, there wouldn't be much point in playing."

WHILE OUR WOMEN'S team was doing well, I was also going full speed in mixed doubles, partnering with my husband. Brent and I first played the fast-paced two-person format at the Continental Cup. That event was modelled after golf's Ryder Cup and pitted teams from North America against the rest of the world. There were three different formats: four-person team play, skins and mixed doubles.

We hit it off in mixed doubles. After the discipline had been added to the Olympics in 2018, we took it more seriously, hoping to get to the Games. In three Canadian championships—2018, 2019 and 2021—we played well enough to finish in the top 10, but nothing beyond that. Both Brent and I gave our four-player teams more attention than the mixed doubles, and we always faced conflicts when we played in the Brier and Scotties. And there was also the rule (which I've mentioned before) that if you made it to the Olympics as part of a men's or women's team,

DREAM BIG

you couldn't play in mixed doubles. (That regulation has been dropped in recent years.) So we didn't have a lot of incentives to continue.

However, we both had a sense that we could achieve something bigger as a two-player team. We were both accomplished players and multiple-time Canadian and world champions—and we thought the same way when we were on the ice. It seemed like a perfect fit.

In 2023, that proved right. We went to Sudbury, Ontario, for the Canadian championship, and when I first stepped on the ice, I got that feeling that this was going to be our time. Sure enough, we went through the competition undefeated, making lots and lots of great shots and rarely getting into trouble.

In the playoffs we got through the quarter-final and semi-final and faced Jocelyn and her husband, Brett Gallant, in the final. We won that game 9–4, scoring five points in the final end to seal the win and become Canadian champions.

We advanced to the world championship, which that year was played in Gangneung, South Korea, where I'd played the women's world championship in 2009. The mixed doubles world championship was relatively new, having started in 2008. No Canadian team had won the gold, and we weren't able to do it either. We played well in the round robin but were upended in the semifinal by the US team.

That run with Brent was so special. It was the first time we were able to share the joy of winning. He'd been there for me when I'd won with my women's team, and I'd done the same for him when his men's rink won. But to win a championship together was extra special.

ROCK STAR

WHEN THAT SEASON ended, I took some time to consider my future with my women's team. I knew in my heart that I wanted to keep playing. The young players had instilled a level of excitement in me, and I was still loving every part of curling—from the practices to the workouts to the games to seeing friends and fans in every part of the country and the world.

Mackenzie decided to take a break from curling and pursue other things in her life. So the four of us kept going, with a goal of trying to improve on what had been a stellar first season. The other three also wanted me to consider staying with them for the full four-year Olympic cycle and taking another run at making the Games. I wouldn't commit to that, but I didn't rule it out.

We started our second year as we had our first, winning the opening Grand Slam event of the season, the Tour Challenge. The good play continued, and because of a change put in by Curling Canada, we knew at the start of the season we would be in the Scotties. Instead of a wild-card playdown just a few days before the Canadian championship started, Curling Canada introduced a pre-qualification system based on the previous year's performance. We'd played well enough to earn one of those spots, and it made life much easier in so many ways, especially scheduling. We knew we'd be playing the week of the Scotties and also that we didn't need to play at the provincial playdowns. Which was good and bad for me. I loved playing in the provincial championship. We didn't get to play in Manitoba very often, but we did, of course, in provincials. That was where our friends and family could come and support us as well as a place where we could connect with fans who had cheered for us for so many years. I missed that interaction and having the opportunity to say thank you.

As the season went on, retirement entered my mind. I still wasn't sure about leaving the game, but I knew I had to consider it. I never wanted to fizzle out or play at a level where I couldn't compete with the best. I always thought there would come a time when I wouldn't want to practise as much, or when I'd grow tired of the competitions. But that hadn't happened. I still loved curling as much as I ever had.

That all changed when we took a trip to Japan to play an event in Karuizawa. I fell in love with Japan the first time we played there. I loved everything about the culture, the people and the food, and so it was easy to say yes when we were invited to compete. My three teammates had never been there, so they left early to spend some time playing tourist.

Normally I would have joined them, but I felt I couldn't leave my daughters. I wanted to be with Skyla and Isabella and be a mother. Instead, I left at the last minute and got there just in time to curl.

Right after I arrived, I got word that both girls were sick, Skyla especially so. It rattled me, and for the first time in my curling career, I wasn't present when my daughters needed me. I couldn't focus on our games because I wanted to be at home, to take care of them and be their mother. At that moment I felt I didn't belong on the curling ice but back in Canada, where I could help my girls get better.

Not surprisingly, we didn't play well in the event and lost out early. I changed my flight so I could get home sooner, leaving a country I adored. That was the moment when I started reflecting on whether it was time to stop curling—at least four-player curling. I knew where my heart was. My family always came before curling, but now it had really sunk in that I needed to be where my family was. It was time.

We had played well and enjoyed a really good season. We had just won a Grand Slam, and I felt like I was playing as well as I had ever played. I had a conversation with Brent and told him I thought I could play one more season but didn't know if I could do two more. In two years, Bella would be in high school.

There was also my mother, Gramma Carol, as she was known on tour, who gave so much of her time to watch the girls when I was competing all over the world. She was now 80, and while I know she would never refuse to stay with her granddaughters, it was asking a lot.

From a team standpoint, playing one more year wasn't fair to the other three either. If I played one more year and ended my career in the spring, that would leave them just a few months before the Olympic trials in November. My decision really came down to either playing for two more years or ending it. I waffled back and forth on it, waking up one day and being certain I wanted to retire and then changing my mind the next day. It was the hardest choice I'd ever had to make.

In January, I knew I had to decide. If I was going to leave the game, I had to give my friends and family a head's up so they could come and watch us at the Scotties or the Players' Championship. Those would be the two final events I would play. Time was running out.

Finally, I made up my mind and felt comfortable with my

DREAM BIG

decision. I told my teammates just before the Scotties that I would be retiring, and they were fully supportive. They could understand my reasons because growing up in their careers, they'd had mothers who had supported them as they became world-class curlers, and they knew I wanted to help my daughters pursue whatever their dreams were. I don't think any of Karlee, Emily or Lauren was disappointed or upset. They were fully behind me. Lauren expressed it best when she told me all three were just honoured to share the ice with me during my final games. I will never forget how it made me feel . . . loved. Lauren has always had the ability to make everyone around her feel loved. I will forever be grateful for that.

The Scotties gave us an almost fairy-tale ending. We played in the final, and it came down to last rock. Just as I had done my entire career, I was dialed in during the last game. I wanted to win for the other three players, but it just didn't happen. They took the loss well, and for me, it was an honour to end my career with them.

Up in the stands, my family watched as I threw my last shots. My sister, her husband and my niece came. One of my best friends, Tina Jones, flew back from Hawaii to attend the final. Mark Britt, my friend who worked at Fairmont and had placed a bet on us early in our career, was there too. So was Viktor, my former coach. He had returned to Canada to coach for Curling Canada. He gave me a hug and said he was so emotional he couldn't talk. Many of the crew members from TSN came over to wish me well. During the broadcast of the game, TSN showed a feature they had put together from many of the great players I'd met and competed against over the last 25 years, giving me their best and telling me how I had affected their careers and the game itself. Brent was standing with one arm around Skyla and the other around Bella, each in their Manitoba jerseys with "Jones" on the back, and of course my mom, Carol, was there. Mom was always there, right from my first rock at the St. Vital Curling Club with my dad to my final rock at the Scotties. And I know my dad was there, telling me, "Ya done good, kid." I could feel his presence. My dad had a watery eye whenever he watched me play, and all week at the Scotties my eye wouldn't stop watering, to the point it was raw. It reminded me of my dad, and when I felt the tear run down my face, I could feel him smiling with pride. I was going to miss this special connection with him, but I knew the connection was so deep it would always be there.

It was all overwhelming, and for the first time since my junior days, I cried a bit on the ice. This time, the tears were not for a game I'd lost but for a sport that had changed my life in so many ways. How lucky was I.

I still had the Players' Championship a few weeks later, where again friends and family came to support me and say goodbye, including my baby group and Dawn McEwen, who flew in to sit on the bench for my final game. That meant the absolute world to me. Kaitlyn was also there with her new team and gave me a hug when the game was over. Jill sent messages wishing she could be there.

I always thought I would miss the physical act of curling the most when I retired, but I came to realize I would miss the people and the fans more. Hearing their stories, feeling the impact we were making, was more than I could have ever dreamed.

DREAM BIG

One story stands out. A young girl told me I had signed a picture for her years before, where I told her to "dream big." She told me she was a foster child and had moved to different homes over the years, but she always kept that picture on her desk. She didn't have a lot of people who believed in her, but I did. She looked at that picture as she studied, she dreamed big and she had just been accepted into medical school. I was so proud of her.

I never dreamed that doing what I loved to do would have such an impact. I genuinely cared about all the fans and people in curling. I would sign as many autographs as I could and tried to stay until everyone had left. I feel it is our responsibility as athletes, but I also always looked at it as a privilege. Not many people go through life being asked for an autograph or a selfie. It is an honour not to be taken for granted.

Now it was time to look to the future—to try my next adventure, or adventures. You need to dream big! Brent and I had decided to purchase the Barrie/Collingwood Weed Man franchise from Brent's parents, who had run it for 40 years. The company was a big part of his life, and we wanted to keep it in the family. We also both have an entrepreneurial mindset and were super excited to take what we learned on the curling ice to our own business. This new chapter was beyond exciting.

I also always had a dream of being in the broadcast booth and never thought it would happen. Over the years, Sportsnet made me feel wanted and invited me to be a guest commentator so I would be ready to step into the booth when the time was right. They took a chance on me, and I loved every second. I am excited to be in the booth providing analysis for the game I love so much. It is hard for me to believe that the shy little girl I once was is now a commentator on national television.

With curling coming to an end and my mom living in Winnipeg, we also wanted to find a way to continue the deep relationship the girls have with Gramma Carol. I was offered the opportunity to work at Princess Auto, a Winnipeg-based company, in a senior role, and I jumped at it. I always want to be a role model for Isabella and Skyla, and this move will allow them to see another side of me. They know I am a lawyer, but for most of their lives curling was front and centre. Now they can see me as part of an executive team. As I always say, dream anything and everything! And as Brent reminds me, we are definitely living life to the fullest, even if it is complicated.

19

A CLEAR MIND,
AN UNBURDENED HEART

LOOKING BACK ON my life, I realize just how much curling has given me. We had many great wins, championship titles and remarkable shots. And the frustrating losses were important too. But the gift wasn't so much about those things. It was about how the sport made me the person I am today.

I grew up an extremely shy girl who wanted to be the absolute best at everything I did. No one ever pushed me to be better. In fact, it was quite the opposite. My parents were supportive and proud, but they never tried to make me do anything. I was the one who was hard on myself, putting on the pressure to get better. Not just at curling, but at everything in my life. That's what everyone wanted from me, I believed. At times I had no idea what—or who—I wanted to be. Not a clue about what I wanted from life. I was just so focused on doing well for everybody else. I wanted to make everyone happy and proud of me. For years, I didn't realize that's what I did and how I thought.

Curling changed everything. It gave me a place where I felt I belonged. It took me from being a shy girl to a confident woman, partner and mother. I became part of a team, and I learned to open up and share my feelings with my teammates. That may have been one of the toughest lessons I ever had to learn. But it was also the most important. It was about trust, about no longer being afraid to feel vulnerable.

I also gained confidence in being a leader—someone who wasn't afraid to speak out and make decisions that I thought were right. Trust me, it wasn't easy. For a long time, I tried not to be the decision-maker because making a choice might upset one of my teammates. Gradually, however, I realized that my teammates, business associates and friends often looked to me for help. They were expecting me to make a decision, and they valued it.

Curling made all this happen. It's given me recognition and honours beyond my wildest expectations. I was awarded the Order of Manitoba, the highest honour for residents of my home province. I was also fortunate to receive this award from King Charles III (then Prince Charles) himself. I also received the Meritorious Service Medal from the Governor General of Canada. And as I was completing this book, I was told I would be honoured with the King Charles III Coronation Medal, created to recognize outstanding individuals who have made a significant contribution both to their local communities and to Canada. These honours make me beyond proud and exceptionally humbled to be included with so many great Manitobans and other Canadians.

Curling has given me confidence I never thought I would

A CLEAR MIND, AN UNBURDENED HEART

have. The more I played the game, the more I loved it. It was the place where I could channel my drive to improve. I was a girl who loved to throw rocks up and down the sheet. I put everything I had into the game, and as I got better, my confidence grew. I remember back to when we first started working with Cal Botterill, our sports psychologist. Cal told me to play the game with a clear mind and an unburdened heart. And when I lacked the confidence or mindset to think I could achieve greatness, he always reminded me, "Why not you?"

At first, I didn't really understand what he meant. I'm 100 percent focused when I'm on the ice, so isn't that the same as a clear mind? What's an unburdened heart? But I wasn't looking at curling from a broader perspective. I was thinking it was all about the shots and the sweeping and the scoreboard.

It was when I met my husband, Brent, that I truly understood what Cal's words to me meant. An unburdened heart means feeling confident in myself, feeling secure in who I am as a person. It means being full of joy with everything I have in life and not burdened by trying to do something—everything—for someone else. It means doing it for me. I constantly worried about everybody but myself—my team, my coaches, my family, my job. I was always in last place, and I was OK with that, as though I didn't care. But Brent loved me for who I was. He loved everything about me, from my smile to my annoying habits. He looked at me and saw *Jennifer* and not *Jennifer Jones the curler*. For the first time in my life, I could be just me without ever second-guessing what that meant.

I did (and I do) enjoy doing things for people, but my reasons weren't right. Brent showed me that I can be a giving person and still feel comfortable in *why* I am a giver. He taught me that I can get great joy out of doing things for him and for us. To me, that's what an unburdened heart means. The feeling grew when I had Isabella and again with Skyla. Without my family, I am not sure I'd be the person I am today.

Brent is a master at filtering out noise and listening only to the voices that matter. He would never let the opinion of a stranger affect him or his heart, especially some comment on social media, where a person can hide behind a fake identity. I am still not there, but he helped me realize what is important and how to protect my heart from outside sources. He has also shown me how slowing down and taking the time to enjoy the little moments in life are the most important things—the magic of life.

Isabella has shown me how tenderness and kindness will fill your cup. Being empathetic and putting yourself in someone else's shoes is key to being a great friend and a great leader. Bella looks everyone in the eyes with genuineness and shows the people in her life that they are loved. She also exemplifies courage and seeking out life's next adventure and understands that change is a part of life, to be embraced. I like to think I have always been open to change, but Isabella definitely has more courage than anyone I have ever met, and she makes me stronger.

Skyla has shown all of us the power of laughter. I always say she is a natural leader whom people gravitate toward. She is spicy and soft and reminds us all to be goofy and never grow up and become a pessimist, to always remember our childhood sense of dreaming and believing. Skyla reminds me to smile and laugh

A CLEAR MIND, AN UNBURDENED HEART

and always be resilient. As she always says, "We can do anything if we work hard and never give up." My family has helped me to grow into a person who enjoys every moment, lives life to the fullest and is grateful for every single second I have on this planet. I am so lucky.

As I reflect on the meaning of Cal Botterill's wise words, I realize it's about being in the moment, being OK with any results and knowing that your best was always going to be good enough. When I was at the 2022 Olympics, and when I was playing in the bubble during Covid, I didn't have a clear mind or an unburdened heart because I was trying to figure out what everybody else needed in that crazy situation. I wanted to make them happy, to make them play well. And I didn't really balance their needs with what I needed. I never made myself a priority. It was just too hard to reach an equilibrium between "others" and "myself." We were in different places, and because I couldn't find that clear path, I didn't have an unburdened heart. I felt weighed down, and no matter how hard I tried, I couldn't discard that feeling. I think that weight—that burden—affected my performance.

A clear mind and an unburdened heart mean chasing *your* dreams, doing what *you* love to do. Yes, you can do those things for other people and with other people, but do them so you bring joy to yourself.

That's what I want for Isabella and Skyla. I don't want them to feel like they have to do, or to be, everything for everybody. I want them to chase their dreams and go after what they want and always have a "Why not me?" mindset. And if they do, it's all I could ever ask because I know it will bring them happiness.

ROCK STAR

Many people said I looked different after I had Isabella. I think that was because I was unburdened; I was with my family, who supported me no matter what, who lifted me up when I was down, who made it so that I never felt pressured to be anything other than myself. They loved me for everything that I was and wasn't. They loved me for *me*, and they taught me how to love myself. They also showed me a different perspective and helped me to grow as a person.

From that point forward, I think, I've been authentically myself and living a joyful, unburdened life. That's what curling has given me—the best possible gift. I finally believe, with everything inside of me, "Why not me?"

I hope everyone can live their lives with a clear mind and an unburdened heart. We get only one life to live, and from my experience, having a clear mind and an unburdened heart is the key to being a great mother, friend, partner and leader. Ultimately, it's the key to happiness and fulfillment.

Thank you, curling, for showing me the path toward true happiness.

ACKNOWLEDGEMENTS

I WOULD LIKE to express my deepest gratitude to my family for their unwavering support throughout the writing of this book but also throughout my life and my curling and professional journey. Which was a lot! For always keeping up with my crazy ideas and grounding me at the same time.

To my daughters, Isabella and Skyla, for embracing our crazy life and hotel homes with enthusiasm and joy and for making my life so much richer than I ever thought possible. For inspiring me to be better and to always chase my dreams, even if it meant sacrifices for my girls. I hope we have inspired you to always chase your dreams and happiness. To my husband, Brent, for being steadfast in my corner and believing in me with everything inside of him. For loving me and our challenging and complicated life and accepting that when I ask twice it is already going to happen. My stepson, Wil, for welcoming me into his world and for supporting the chaos. You remind us not to sweat the small stuff . . . or the big stuff, really. Just be chill. To my sister, Heather, for being my number one fan and willing to ride the curling roller coaster with me for so many years, and her husband, Jeff, and daughter, Kendall, for putting up with her "stress." To my mom, Carol, without whom none of this would

ACKNOWLEDGEMENTS

be possible. You were my first and greatest role model for how to navigate the world as a woman with integrity, empathy and strength. From always telling me I could do anything, to being a "granny nanny" for our girls, you are the best person I know in every possible way. Known as Gramma Carol on tour, you made our girls feel loved in their hotel homes and allowed Brent and me to chase our dreams. You really are magic. Thank you and love you forever, Mom. To my dad, who loved the game of curling and his girls more than anyone I know. He taught me to be grateful for the opportunity to do what I love and to never be scared to lose. To embrace all that is good in life. I miss you every day, Dad, but know that your love has lived on in all of us. I am also so grateful to my extended family for expanding my small nuclear family into a big, blended, wondrous village.

Thank you, Anne, Mike, Emma and Amelia, for making your home ours and for loving the girls as if they were a part of your family. For always being there to help with Isabella and Skyla without question and to help me figure out logistics, which was not easy!

This book would not have been possible without my incredible teammates over the years who stood by me and allowed me to share the stage with them. I love you all—it was an absolute privilege. A special thank you to Dawn for flying to Toronto for my last game and sitting on the bench when the last rock was thrown. This will always be one of my favourite memories and meant so much to me. Forever teammates.

My beautiful friends who always treated me as Jen and made me feel accepted for who I was . . . thank you! You are all incredible women who inspire me to be better in every way

ACKNOWLEDGEMENTS

and remind me that I can do anything. You are brilliant, kind, compassionate and driven, and I am so grateful my girls have you to look up to. You even supported me in curling when many of you have never even been on curling ice. The sense of lifelong friendship and acceptance brought me more strength than you will ever know, and I will be forever grateful.

The world is a better place thanks to people who want to develop and lead others and are willing to share their gifts and mentor and support other people. To my brilliant coaches, thank you for always answering my call. For inspiring me to push myself and the limits and to never be satisfied with the status quo.

A special thanks to Jeff and my publishing team for believing in this story and championing it to anyone who would listen. To Bob Weeks for his dedication to shaping the manuscript and helping me get the words on paper so that it would be an interesting read for all of you.

Finally, to my fans for their support over the years and who made my dream so much bigger than I could ever imagine, and to the readers for choosing to read my story. That, in itself, is an incredible compliment.